HUON WRITES

ISBN–print: 978-0-6459137-9-8

Published by Ashwood Publishing in collaboration
with MKoach Design.

ashwoodpublishing.com.au
mkoach.com

For enquiries please email: info@ashwoodpublishing.com.au
or meng@mkoach.com

Editors: Susan Young and Meng Koach
Cover and book design: MKoach Design

Cover art: Cassie Sullivan.
Cassie Sullivan is a lutruwita / trouwerner First Nations artist based on Melukerdee Country in lutruwita / Tasmania. She has a responsive art practice that crosses disciplines of moving image, photography, writing, sound, installation and printmaking. She works with a deeply considered process-driven practice that prioritises an engagement with Country. Within her creative and cultural practice, she works to constantly question what can be imbued through materiality to give voice to complex identities.

HUON WRITES

AN ANTHOLOGY FROM THE TASMANIAN SOUTH

CONTENTS

INTRODUCTION

Like many things, *Huon Writes* started in Cygnet's Red Velvet Lounge. We were having a coffee and got talking about how, if you spend any length of time there, you constantly run into people who are writing something, making something, organising something, in diverse and creative ways. We decided to produce *Huon Writes* to help celebrate and promote our amazing writing community. We hope it will become a regular anthology that publishes emerging writers alongside established authors, strengthens connections, and lets visitors and locals alike read a variety of writing on whatever writers in the Huon are thinking and writing about.

With this in mind, we didn't ask for a particular theme, but inevitably, the sublime natural environment we enjoy here came up again and again. Lutruwita Tasmania is an extraordinary place, and it insists on having a voice in us and in what we create. Not just a few lyrical references to the sweep of the sea or the glow of the light; in the growing body of Tasmanian literature, Tasmanian characters get out there in the cold and wet; they clear land and grow crops; they hunt, in the sea and on land; they pass by carnage every day, as we all do, as they go about their lives. The place itself – its beauty, its isolation, its history – is the thrumming bass note running in the background always. Modern culture on this island is so recent, its ancient culture so assaulted, that we are still wrestling with the deep moral question facing anyone who lives here – how to create a way of life, not just as individuals but as a society, that treads lightly and preserves what we have here.

The summer and autumn of 2023–24 were the Huon Valley's driest for many years. Whole hillsides browned off as trees became desperate for water, and as we compile this anthology, in late winter, hay is three or four times the normal price. We're not used to this here in our fecund green valley, and it's obviously on the minds of our authors: heat and dry strikes a warning note in several of the stories. Kate Kruimink's narrator, arriving in a heatwave at a family get-together in one of those new, grey houses in a subdivided paddock, laments the 'slow retreat of all winter'. Zoe Davidson, setting off to look for new horizons in Melbourne, leaves a Huon Valley parched from a summer that's 'drier than ever before'. Matthew Evans writes of watching the forest opposite his home die of thirst.

Some days, you can drive along the road here and every new curve presents a view to feed the soul, and many people feel a strong obligation to reciprocate. Lisa Litjens reminisces lyrically on walking on kunanyi, but also on continual actions to preserve it from invasive development. Matthew Evans has made an entire new career on building a life that is connected to land and community here in the Huon and, in the process, has delved deeply into questions around how to farm in ways that enrich and preserve the land. Wren Fraser Cameron has spent the last forty years campaigning to preserve both the natural environment of Lune River and its history, and those struggles, too, feature in her meditation on the way history shapes our lives. The past is not another country; it is in Country, walking with us, and we become part of it even as we move forward through life.

On seeing Bob Brown's name on our list of authors, you may have expected a piece about environmental campaigns. Bob does make a passing reference to the weather being unseasonably warm, but for us he's written a gentle, very personal story of a morning spent looking for a lost lamb. It's a story of partnership, care and community. Winsor Dobbin – who is no slouch in helping build community himself, with his famously convivial wine tasting dinners – offers quite a different sort of writing in an article on the developing wine industry in the valley. David L Hume takes us to a different side of life in the region in a story of outsiders, of no fixed address, who find refuge and freedom in the bush. Marjorie Gadd's protagonist, Tezza, also celebrates the kind of life you can build out in nature, up in the hills – but a supply trip to Huonville is about to change his life. And maybe there's more to the flat part of the

Huon Valley than meets the eye: in Isaac Gee's story of a night at the Midwinter Festival, the thin winter air holds a fey sense of mystery.

Like any successful rural community, our region thrives on people building connections with one another and with the place they live in. It's one of the things many newcomers to the valley come for and, once they get here, help develop. Matthew Evans notes that in the best type of community, people rely on each other; in Bob Brown's story it's the daughter of some friends who offers to adopt an orphaned lamb. Zoe Davidson writes of a disconnect to nature and feeing adrift in Melbourne, but it's striking how much underlying confidence being grounded in the Huon has given her: she knows these paddocks, this dam; follows their changes, walks confidently in the dew-drenched grass; she faces the big city secure in her own values. Kate Kruimink's unhappy narrator has fared less well in life, and has become so alienated that she can hardly bear to reach down and be handed a relative's new baby – but somehow she does, and is drawn, at least a little, towards hope.

We've been thrilled at the response from our writers. People have been overwhelmingly positive about the project, and authors have carved out time in their busy schedules to write for it. They've written an eclectic selection of stories – fiction and non-fiction, longer and shorter, some literary and some simple and direct – that give an insight into what it means to live in this place. We hope you enjoy this *Huon Writes* anthology, and that it's the first of many more to come. **HW**

PITFALLS IN THE NIGHT

Bob Brown

Just before the Randalls Bay turnoff, you can look out over the undulating pastures of the Thomases' farm, down the widening valley to the bay and the Huon River estuary beyond. People stop there to admire the view, and on an aurora night they gather there in hushed communion as they look out at the Southern Lights in awe. Down at the shoreline, the gentle beach and shallow bay have taught generations of children to swim and row and sail and see the wonder in a rockpool or a weathered tree trunk, and fair weather or foul, people walk and swim there for the peace it brings. Randalls is a special place.

Bob Brown has published extensively about environmental and political issues and is famous (or infamous, depending on one's point of view) for his sustained and courageous environmental activism. Here, he shares the story of a different interaction with his environment, in a simple, heartwarming tale of partnership and care.

'You do come home!' I said as Paul came in the door after dark, and I got him a beer from the fridge. He had been searching the nooks and crannies in the far top paddock for a lamb that had separated from its mother. 'I wonder if the wedge-tailed eagle got it?' I asked. The eagles sometimes take a dead or sickly lamb.

In the lambing season Paul goes around his flock every morning and evening. I like to tag along and stroke the ewes' brows while he attends to any birthing problems. So, next morning, we headed off to do the rounds, ending up in the far top paddock.

Though this was the second morning of spring by the calendar, there was no frost, fog or dew. It was unseasonably warm, with hardly a cloud in the sky. A few white flecks of snow remained on the distant wilderness mountains. Paul's steep-terrain farm overlooks the sea, and the rising sun threw long shadows across the hillsides from the skyline trees. As we walked up to the furthest corner of the farm an eagle came out of the western woods and floated 50 metres over our heads, hardly a feather moving in its effortless morning surveillance flight. It turned north and disappeared over the ridge.

We walked back down the gully that drains the paddock. The gully starts with a high, marshy flat and ends, 500 metres downhill, in a small creek running through a copse of blackwood trees and ferns and then into a cool, deep green pond. Most of the watercourse is grassy but here and there, since the earth-binding forest was removed more than a century ago, holes appear where the creek has eroded underground for a little way before surfacing again.

Paul reckoned the lamb might have ended up in one of those holes.

It hadn't. However, our search led to a miraculous rescue.

'I'll need your help!' Paul suddenly called to me as he knelt and reached to full stretch below the paddock. I hurried over to where, with his own eagle's eye, he had spotted white wool in a deep shadowy hole amongst the clumps of reeds in the gully.

Paul hauled a ewe up from the depths. Her head appeared above the ground and, clutching the thick winter wool of her flank, I helped him lift her back onto the paddock. She stood stock-still, silent, dripping some mud and bewildered by her underground experience. But she hadn't been alone. 'Her lamb must be down there too,' said Paul as he lay flat on his belly and reached deeper into the black cavern beneath. And there it was.

Paul lifted high a muddy but very lively lamb. Within seconds the lamb was under its mother for a revival drink and then, in the warm morning sunlight, the rescued pair headed downhill to rejoin their flock in greener pastures.

During the night the unsuspecting lamb had fallen into the hole. In my mind's eye I could see the ewe desperately searching for her lamb bleating below – and suddenly falling in too. There they would have stayed and died had it not been for our search for the first lamb, whose own minor miracle was about to unfold.

High up on the hill, near the thistle patch where a giant eucalypt had fallen in the cyclonic storm of 2009, Paul found his lost lamb. It was thin but in good health. He took it to its ewe, now on the next hill, but she rejected it. Luckily, Paul had a more enthusiastic mother-in-waiting called Billie.

Billie is the twelve-year-old daughter of friends near town. She had telephoned a fortnight earlier to put in an order for any female lamb that was orphaned. So Paul took the lamb back home and called Billie to let her know that it was needing her care. The lucky lamb spent the rest of the sunlight hours keeping us entertained – not least when it jumped up onto the office couch to show off its ancestral link with mountain goats.

Our friends arrived before dark, and Billie was delighted. She bottle-fed the lamb with the skill of a veteran and took it off to its own greener pastures. Not every lamb spends one night abandoned beside wildlife-filled woods and the next in a garden home with an attentive new mother.

There are pitfalls in the night, but the sun never fails to rise, and fate works its surprises in both directions. **HW**

On Leaving the Huon Valley

Zoe Davidson

It's an old story: young people leaving Tasmania for better opportunities, or just to expand their horizons, on the mainland. Zoe Davidson's parents did the same in their time – but they came back, and then it was Zoe's turn. As she makes her own flight, Zoe is acutely aware of the birds: the plovers who, as we all know, persevere and breed in the face of multiple hazards, and the battle-scarred birds of Melbourne, whose rubbish-snagged feet speak of humanity's careless trashing of nature. She returns home to find the new plover family wheeling above green, refreshed pastures – for now.

As a child, Zoe Davidson lived in NSW and Malaysia before settling down in the Huon Valley. In 2021, she won the Australian Association of Writing Programs/ Voiceworks Sudden Fiction Prize, and in 2023, collected a second prize in the RD Walsh Writing for the Environment Award. Her writing focuses on the human-wrought destruction of the environment, whether fictional or very real. She currently lives in Naarm / Melbourne.

It's late summer, and the beauty of the Huon Valley fades into heat-stricken shades of brown and palest gold. The creek that runs through our property has become a dusty path; the little frogs that croaked from its banks have vanished. This summer is different to the last, drier than ever before. I know the Valley, and this is strange for it.

The sun streaming through the window feels like it's going to burn my leg. I'm sitting with my suitcase open in front of me, clothes half-packed and books (do I really need so many books?) piled beside it. I've been sorting my things all day, deciding what I'll take with me to start my new life. I need a break.

I take a pair of long gumboots from beside the door and go for a walk. The heat is worse outside as the sun bears down – perfect snake weather. The uncut grass in the paddocks is long, seed-heads tickling against my legs.

The plovers are at it again on the dam. A pair of them, Mum and Dad to be, have built a nest in the centre of the dam, beside the muddy puddle that's all that's left of the water. It's a couple of leaves and some sticks in an untidy arrangement on the exposed clay – I'd thought it was debris that had gathered when the water dropped, until the first green-speckled egg appeared. Last count, they'd laid three. There might be more, but they're too protective to let anyone close enough to check. One of them is crouched over the eggs now, while the other gives me the stink-eye from where it's perched on the dam wall.

I give it a little wave. It responds with a low warning squawk, startling a rosella out of the tree above me.

In a few days' time I'm going to be in a city I've never set foot in before. Excitement bubbles in my stomach at the thought of leaving – finally! It feels like getting my life started.

Even my parents have come around to the idea. They're both returning Tasmanians who had their own adventures before coming back and settling down. They might not be thrilled at seeing me go, but they can't argue that they didn't do the same when they were my age.

I'm going to fit right into Melbourne, I think. No more hours spent mucking out duck pens or patching up fences for me. I'll be a city girl having adventures.

I can't wait.

I've been to big cities before, I tell myself. I've been to Sydney and Canberra and Singapore and Kuala Lumpur. As a child. With my parents.

It's completely different as an adult arriving alone. I'm overwhelmed and disorientated, and a little bit disgusted with how dirty everything is. There's a plastic bag rolling along the footpath and rubbish spilling out of the bins. Street cleaners drive along in their cleaning machines, but grime quickly accumulates in the wake of their spinning brushes.

I almost get run over as I'm crossing at the traffic lights. The green man light is on and I'm walking behind a group of other pedestrians when a car cuts around the corner. It scoots between us and I have to back up to avoid getting hit. And they say Tasmanian drivers are reckless!

I walk past the door to my hostel twice before I find it. If Maps wasn't swearing black and blue that the place was here, I would never have kept looking. It's an almost invisible door between two busy shops, marked only by a small sign. It opens into a long corridor which leads into a small room with an elevator. A piece of paper stuck above the elevator button reads: Push 3 for reception.

Ok, I'm in the right place.

The receptionist is friendly in an efficient manner, handing me my key and a little card with my room number written on it – which is good, because after repeating it back to her, it immediately vanishes out of my brain.

I get to my room and unpack my stuff, stacking the books beside my bed. My single window looks out over the street. Everything and anything, five minutes away. Shops and restaurants, cars and trams; people of all races and genders and fashion styles walking along. I feel giddy watching it all go past.

The window won't open more than a crack, probably because I'm on the fifth floor, but I open it as much as possible and take a quick video of the city below me.

I send it to my mum. Look at me I'm in Melbourne. I can do this.

Every five minutes a train goes past and rattles the whole room. And the cute little trams let out cute little squeals as they slow for the traffic lights. At some point around 2 am there was yelling on the street outside – drunks getting into a fight.

I tell myself the sounds of the city aren't that much worse than the sounds of the countryside at night. The trains could be a storm lashing the trees outside my window at home. The trams and traffic could be the rooster crowing at the moon, the possums fighting, the scratch of rats in the ceiling. But the light coming from behind the curtains is changing from the orange tint of streetlights to the pale grey of early morning sun, and I haven't slept a wink. It's no use: I may as well get up.

It's early, but the city is wide awake and the streets are bustling. Businesspeople talking into their phones, tired-looking parents with babies in strollers, goth couples with matching blue hair. People everywhere, going about their business, yet nobody talking to anyone. It makes sense, there's not enough hours in the day to talk to everyone I meet, yet I have to keep biting my tongue. The small-towner in me demands to make polite conversation.

I stop myself from telling a guy off as he dumps a cigarette butt into the bushes. How they can stay so green after treatment like that, I have no idea. Decades of selective propagation, most likely.

On my early morning walks at home, my only companions were hungry ducks and the occasional sleepy wallaby. Everything here feels so artificial, I can't picture myself ever getting used to it. Yet plenty of people do – more of us are living in cities than ever before. What effect is being so far from nature having on us, and our collective psychology?

Back in my room, I make myself a cup of tea. I take a sip, then almost spit it out. Even the water tastes different here. It's stale, with the chemical undertones of fluoride. The taste lingers in my mouth after the tea has faded, a stark reminder of how far I am from home.

The place I'm staying at isn't far from the river, so on my fourth day in Melbourne I go for a walk along the riverbank. It's a nice atmosphere. There's a few garden beds and some trees; music playing faintly from speakers.

I buy a muffin and sit on a bench with a good view of the water. Seagulls and pigeons flutter around, harassing river goers. A pigeon lands near my foot. It preens itself a little, fluffing its wings up. It looks at my muffin, its eyes big and hopeful.

I break off a bit and hold it out in my hand. The pigeon limps a few steps towards me but won't come any closer. Its right foot seems to be injured.

The whole foot is swollen and there's something trailing from it.

I toss the cake on the ground and the pigeon dives in. Its foot is at a better angle now, and I can see what's causing the problem – there's a bit of plastic string tangled around its toe, cutting off the circulation.

If it was a chook at home with a leg like that, I'd grab it and cut the plastic off. But there's no way this pigeon is letting me get close enough for that.

I pay more attention to the birds as I walk back. There's a little brown myna, its foot so tangled that it's functionally a club. There's another pigeon missing toes, and a little mudlark as well. So many ruined feet, just because humans can't clean up their trash.

I shouldn't have been surprised. I've seen plenty of what happens when humans don't give a shit about the world around them. The number of dead animals on the sides of the roads back home is evidence enough. But I just can't get away from it here.

What are we really losing, when we cut down the forests and pave them over? More than just a loss to our planet; I think we're losing some part of our selves. We're so disconnected.

I miss the Valley, having nature in the backyard, hissing and squawking if I dared get too close. Living on the edge of it all was a privilege. It was grounding, and without it I feel unmoored.

But I am starting to enjoy Melbourne.

After I get used to the crowds, I find them kind of fun. I can go out and be among people all day and yet speak to no-one. It's unsettling, but also freeing, in a way.

I join up for a writers' group. I've tried writers' groups before – some have been great, others, not so much. When I arrive at this one, it's a much larger group than I was expecting, with a real mix of people. There are some older people, but also younger people, and a bunch of twenty-somethings sitting down one end of the table, talking and laughing together. One of them gestures excitedly and I notice they're wearing a rainbow flag wristband. I plonk my laptop down that end as subtly as I can.

Afterwards, the person comes over to me and starts chatting. They noticed we're both wearing the same shoes! I laugh at the coincidence – I almost didn't bring these shoes to Melbourne. They invite me over to meet their friends, and suddenly the five of us are going out to lunch together. We chat about our current writing projects over burgers and kombucha.

I used to travel an hour by bus to a queer youth group as a kid, to form a few friendships that sooner or later fizzled out. We were too scattered to make any real connections.

Here, we compare notes about whose first manuscript was worse and laugh. I could get used to this.

On the way back from the restaurant and we're standing at the traffic lights. The light goes green, and we start to cross. A car comes around the corner, nudging in to see if it can cut through. I turn my head and glare at the driver through the windscreen. They slow to a shameful stop to let us pass.

That's right, I think, show some respect.

And then I'm on a plane again, on my way back home for a visit. As we fly over the island I can see the mountains, the forests, the pale patches of cleared land. A hundred shades of green, at least until the next extreme summer.

Mum picks me up from the airport and we drive back along the familiar roads. Everything seems smaller, somehow. The setting sun tints the clouds with pink as the town gives way to countryside and the four-lane highway becomes a winding road through the trees. The stars come out, bright and visible in a dark sky that's free of light pollution.

As we reach our driveway, Mum slows the car to let a wallaby run past. It skids in panic under the glare of our headlights, then picks itself up and disappears into the undergrowth.

In the morning, I wake up to chooks cackling. Outside, the fog blankets everything in wintery shades of grey and the damp grass squelches under my boots.

There are four plovers strutting across the paddocks. Mum and Dad and two babies, all grown up. The dam is full, their nest deep underwater. The creek runs as if it never stopped, the frogs croaking from its banks.

The hills stretch out before me, green and inviting. **HW**

The Apocalypse of You

Kate Kruimink

Kate's Kruimink's evocative story connects alienation from the environment with social fragmentation as the unhappy Helen makes her way to a family get-together. There's an inchoate sense of wrong in the unfamiliar heat, in Helen's sluggish reluctance, in her sense of disconnect at the changes to her childhood home. She feels alienated from her family, 'all of them enmeshed in the generations of each other, each other's fathers and mothers and sisters and brothers'. She is drawn in, welcomed and embraced – but will have to reach out if she is to connect again.

Kate's first novel, *A Treacherous Country*, won the 2020 *The Australian*/Vogel's Literary Award. It was shortlisted in the Prime Minister's Literary Award for Fiction and longlisted in the UK for the Walter Scott Prize for Historical Fiction. In 2021, she was one of the *Sydney Morning Herald*'s Best Young Novelists. Her second novel, *Heartsease*, was published mid-2024 with Picador. Recently, Kate was the inaugural joint winner of the Weatherglass Books Novella Prize in the UK with her novella, *Astraea*, set on a women's convict ship. She also works as Fiction Editor at *Island* magazine.

In its final days, the year crumpled under a slow heatwave. The sky was a desert, all clouds burnt away. The great black river huddled low into its mud, clinging its atoms together against the thirsty air. I saw it thick and dull through the trees as I drove.

When I was a child, I was more like a little animal than a girl, like a young cat or bird of prey. I used to lurk in the margins of that river, inscribing the flat stones with my wet inhuman prints. The tea-coloured water was cold and clean. Now it looked viscous, like melted tar.

Nothing is as good as it used to be. You can test this, if you like, to prove it wrong, and your test will fail: revisit the finest places of your childhood and expect to summon the same joy back, the same old, wild, amoral joy, the bold love of ice and snow. Only try and summon this splendour back to you as a changed being, a being older and more cynical and abraded, now, by the banal wearing of the days, by the slow retreat of all winter, and see what happens.

Through the trees, the river slopped its belly to the sky. I don't like coming here, where it has not been my home for a long time. Home was once a cold place, wet and green. Fires crackled in blackened hearths, even at this time of year. Mould bloomed on bedroom walls. Out windows, frosted mushrooms nosed shy faces under the smiling moon. Wet-nosed animals grew their furs thick into the crisp midsummer air.

The road sparkled ahead of me, dipped and curved. The flat white tissue paper–wrapped gift on the seat beside me slid. I was in my cocoon of air conditioning, but outside the trees shimmered. Home but not-home. A wondrous loneliness billowed me forward.

An inflatable Santa bobbed over the town hall, his face above his beard cartoonish, black eyes popping in the heat, cheeks perfect red circles. Tinsel Christmas forms glittered sharply above the street, the puddings, the stockings, and the angels bolted to lampposts too hot to touch. They striped the road with their thin shadows. Baffled tourist families huddled in the shade of the pencil pines at the edge of the carpark. They'd have prepared, hearts full of hope, for summer snow and for Antarctic winds whistling north to them over a black ocean. They stood with their down jackets balled in their hands, looking around for something to do. The cafes were closed.

It was the no-man's-land after Christmas and before New Year's, the limp days of anticlimax. I was tired of it. I hadn't liked looking at it in my calendar, at those empty boxes, with a circle only around today. I'd got rid of the calendar, in fact, and now I marked the days passing by watching the light shift across the bright rectangle on my wall, where many years of calendars had hidden the wallpaper from the sun.

I drove slowly, slower than the limit. Then I sped up and slung the car around the roundabout and saw the cops driving towards me. I parked guiltily outside the pub, its plus-sized wreaths bosoming above me from the old veranda. The cops drove by, cool and remote above their slow tyres. I wondered if they had ever felt a sadness this deep into their bone marrow.

The woman in the bakery was like a damp sponge. 'Hot enough?' the man ahead of me asked her, lingering although he had already bought his bread, and she winced. His fingerprints smeared the counter. At the back of the kitchen came the click and the buzz of an oven timer.

'I have to get the pies out,' she told us, and shuffled to the great red grin of the oven to slide her hands into mitts and retrieve a tray of crisp meat pies. My heart thumped like a fist on a door. The man brushed me with his moist body as he left with his loaf of bread. The baker closed the oven and set the pies on a metal bench and came slowly back to me to sell me a family-sized quiche Lorraine. 'My sister's name,' she told me, miserably, looking down at the oven mitts she had forgotten to remove.

'What?'

'Lorraine.'

The car oozed out the other end of town. I knew Lorraine; she'd taught me piano. Her nails used to clatter on the keys.

The sea opened and the road recoiled. Trees closed in on me around corners and then loosened on the straights, brown paddocks unrolling opposite the shining water.

These things were unchanged: the red letterbox, the leaning fence, the cattle ramp bumping me over the threshold between the rest of the world and the place that had been mine. But the old house was now planted with pink and many shades of green, the walls painted blue with white trim. It crouched, cool and well-watered amidst the stretches of brown. As I rattled by, I saw the sprinklers whisking, rhythmic and coordinated as dancers offering their grace to the sky. My old bedroom window was obscured by ferns. I drove on to the new units winking on the brow of the hill and parked my car behind all the other twinkling cars. All the many children, hardened against the sun, shrieked and ducked and ran in their bathers, squirting each other with plastic water pistols. Thin arcs of water glimmered in the light. The children's feet slapped on the hot concrete. The heat lunged at me and my gelid quiche and my little white parcel as I left the car. There was a weak warm splash against my calf.

'Sorry, auntie.' I looked; it was a boy, one of the boys of one of my brothers, I thought, but too big, too tall. 'Didn't mean to get you,' he said, and they scattered again as I traipsed to the door. The wreath was still there, dried willow woven with this and that of red and green.

Through the aluminium-framed window I could see my cousin Pat on the couch, her husband with his arms around her, her head on his shoulder. The little wad of swaddle between them. My heart sank. I'll admit it: I find love embarrassing. I don't want my pillowcases yellowed by the oil of another head. I don't want my waist troubled by hands, my name tender like a sore tongue in someone else's mouth. If everyone wouldn't mind just being quiet, I thought. If everyone wouldn't mind just being quiet and letting me be quiet too, things might be better.

I knocked, slow as molasses. A lesser cousin let me in. It was cold and piney. The plastic tiles were thick underfoot, the air conditioner humming. Every surface was cool grey and looped with silver tinsel. Relatives hovered on these surfaces, cups of tea in their well-meaning hands. The cups had come up from the old house after it was sold. They were so fine I could see the shadows of broad fingers through the sides.

There they were, the relatives, arrayed, all of them enmeshed in the generations of each other, each other's fathers and mothers and sisters and brothers. The Christmas tree was lopsided in the corner, its topmost branch drooping, the star wafting a little, back and forth, in the aircon.

'Oh Helen darlin,' people were saying to me. 'Look it's good of you to come. Shut the door behind you darlin. You're letting the heat in.'

'Letting the cold out,' said the lesser cousin. She took the quiche from me. I stood with the white parcel in my hands. 'Should I warm it up?' the lesser cousin mused, and gave the quiche a jiggle.

The television was on, muted, mounted on the wall. A sensible brunette royal was visiting a school. She was throwing her head back and laughing in the soft English sun. Heels on green turf. Tiny waist. Uniformed children with flowers. Scene change and there she was again, gamely striking a hockey ball with a wooden stick. The tidy teachers applauded, the heavy-blazered girls looked up.

'Another world,' said a grandmother, and, 'You'd think she'd be too thin to have children, but she's done well.'

It was not another world. What was another world was on the couch, Pat and her husband and the new baby cocooned between them. A parallel existence. But Pat looked up at me and said, in defiance of physics, 'Come and have a hold.'

It's not that I wasn't willing to, if asked, but that the shift required felt too great. Like I had to perform a space-time breach to somehow enter their sphere. I looked down at them, Pat and her husband, at the brief moment of a person in their arms.

'You have to do what a new mother says,' someone said to me, and so in the end I stooped through the aeons between us, and Pat rose, helped by the man, and she put the bundle in my arms, and I gave her the white parcel in return.

'Support the head,' she told me. 'Oh, you know how.' And she sat down again and turned over the parcel and opened it slowly. There was a spray of water against the window from outside, the children's bodies darting off beyond the glass, laughing, loose and joyous. I stood holding the baby, the swaddle drooping from my arms like petals, the face there, suddenly, the centre of all things, soft and milky and asleep. The tissue paper of my gift rustled quietly. The baby's lips were pursed and the eyelashes against the cheeks, the nose just a dab, a fine mist of hair like pollen. This child unaware of me. This child giving herself to her sleep in its completeness, in the lack of there being anything else she needed to do or worry about.

'This is lovely,' said Pat, holding up the little green growsuit I'd bought them. 'Ta very much, Helen.'

'She's upset,' said my grandmother. 'Helen, love, are you upset?' I didn't reply. It wasn't relevant. The feral children outside cackled and shouted, their high voices around us like birds. I felt them dancing around and around the new little house, their streams of water, their bold feet, their elbows and knees, their sweet and wild heads. I looked and looked at the baby. Already I was worrying ahead, worrying about myself alone again, tonight, in my own little place, neat and tidy. The bright square on the wall. It was good that the calendar was gone. In the ranks of unhappy days, how could it hold this one day that had, all at once, unfurled a small bud that was quiet and good? **HW**

Tezza

Marjorie Gadd

The Huon Valley lies cupped in the hands of the surrounding mountains, and many people live above the valley itself, revelling in the clean air and mind-expanding views and, importantly, in being above the fog line. Of course, every now and then you have to make your way down a long, winding road and get supplies. In Huonville, the centre of the valley, you'll nearly always meet someone you know; here Marjorie Gadd tells the story of a rather different meeting.

Marjorie Gadd and her husband, Steve Gadd, have spent many years performing, recording and teaching traditional Tasmanian country dance music. Marjorie's 2022 novel, *Golden Valley*, follows a family who move down to the Huon amid the social change of the 1960s and 1970s, and is marked by vivid, complex characterisation and a poetic feeling for place. Marjorie was principal writer in the multi-media productions *Jane Franklin – an Examined Life* and *FIRE*, a history of the 1967 Tasmanian bushfires. As a sixth-generation Tasmanian and long-time resident of southern Tasmania, she has a vital interest in Tasmania's unique and evolving culture.

It was the finest of days. Late summer, early autumn. There'd been no bushfires to speak of. We'd had a cold summer, and now we could relax. I could look out from the veranda into the clear blue sky and see nothing but the tops of hills, the Snowy Range in the distance. The air had thinned out. You could feel the autumn. It's like the air stands up straight and looks around. That column of stillness that says *Hallo, what's going on here?* But the sky's full of birds, and not the pretty ones. The hawks and eagles, the chuck-birds, currawongs, and crows. And then, as if to give you a treat, the grey shrike thrush lifts its head and spreads its beautiful sound across the whole valley. It never fails to move me. Lifts me out of whatever mood I'm in. Reminds me how glorious the world is.

So, there I am, finished me morning coffee and off to the dunny to make a deposit. This dunny has the best view in the valley. That's because I never finished making a door for it. I could sit there for ages, and often do. The seat's made of Huon pine. I got it from an old fella in Franklin. He's lived there all his life and never thrown anything out. I had to convince him that it was going to a good home. It'd been sitting in his back shed for about fifty years. No cracks or splinters. I sanded it back, lightly oiled it, and placed it where it belonged. It's my pride and joy. It's warm and smooth and soft. Huon's a great timber. Me whole house is made of timber. Myrtle, sassafras, celery top, Tassie oak. It's all salvaged from the forestry coupes.

Those bastards just leave it there and burn it. Minor species that's worth a mint. My house is beautiful because of those timbers. The floor's myrtle. The kitchen's celery top. And I've just finished a bookcase made of sassafras.

Anyway, there I am, on the dunny enjoying the most beautiful of days. Just finished making my deposit and a tiger snake decides to pay me a visit. It doesn't slowly slide around my feet. Oh, no, this fella whips his head around the corner and eyeballs me. He's standing up about a foot away from my nose. This has never happened before. He's curious and his little tongue is flicking around and around in all directions. So I just sit. I don't want to make a move. I could reach for the toilet roll but I don't want to give my position away. Where's the dog? I ask myself. I know exactly where she is. She's asleep on the veranda. She's old now and can't be bothered chasing snakes. I've been lucky that she's never been bitten. I contemplate what a snake bite on the nose would be like. Would I lose me nose? I've got some anti-venom in the house, thank god.

I could risk yelling out to the neighbours. There's seven of us living up here on the roof of the valley. Two don't count. They're Vietnam veterans. They're complete lunatics. You won't see them from one Xmas to the next. They don't even talk to each other. Wouldn't turn up to their own funeral.

I could yell out a cooee, and hope someone heard me, but all that would do is agitate this fella. So, I sit there for a million years admiring his perfect snakeness, and suddenly he disappears. I can breathe again.

Right. On with the business of the day. I've got to get down to the valley and do me fortnightly shopping. I want to get there before it gets too busy. Don't like crowds much, although I always run into a few people I know. One of the challenges or delights of living in the valley. I skip the shower and breakfast and make my way down the mountain in me trusty Land Rover. I've had this vehicle since 1997, and it was second-hand when I got it. Just about every part of it has been replaced at some stage. A smart-arse philosopher would ask if it was the same vehicle. Well, it is to me. Aren't many Land Rovers of that vintage around these days. In fact I think it's the only one in the valley.

So, before you know it, I'm shuffling round the stupor-market pushing a trolley. It's a great leveller, the stupor-market. No matter what your station in life, you all look slightly zombiefied. The place is full of tired young mums trailing kids, with looks on their faces that say *I wish I hadn't.* Lots of women think I've got it easy, and would take any opportunity to darn me socks or knit me a beanie. But I'm a wary animal.

Eventually I get out of there. A few smiles and nods, but no conversation. Especially not with the young mums. Women are to be avoided at all costs. Not all my neighbours agree with this policy. Some of the other roof dwellers have experimented with serial monogamy and one's had a whole tribe of sheilas at his place. The mad Viet vets don't count. Not even the possums go near them.

I'm in a hurry to get back home. I want to pay a visit to the gorge. Sometimes you just get a yearning for a particular place. It has a pull on you.

At the back of the mountain the land slopes away and then drops completely. The gorge opens up like the devil's mouth. It cracks the roof in two. It's a wonderful place. The man ferns are about three storeys high. It makes you feel small. At the height of summer, it gets about three hours' sunshine. In winter the frost and snow go undisturbed. There's a waterfall at the top end. Me and the other roof dwellers (apart from the mad bastards) have cleared a pool below it. Some days we make a huge fire and camp down there for a couple of days. Diving in and out of the pool, having a few bongs, drinking Scotch and eating whatever we brought with us. If we run out, there's plenty of wallaby. One of my more agile comrades suggests that we have ritual sex on the winter solstice in our magic grove. Can't see it happening myself. It's too bloody cold.

Then again, there are some females that might be up for it. Every now and then I get visitors. Young women doing research on rare orchids, or the Tasmanian thornbill. 'Can I stay a night or two?' 'Of course! Darling. Be my guest.' They're smart types with muscular bodies. They know the Latin names of flora and fauna and have been to private schools and university. And they're not afraid of roughing it. Before you know it, they're in your bed giving instructions in bullet-point form. I know I'm some sort of trophy fuck for them. But what's a man to do? It's over in a flash and then they disappear. It's nothing like what I had with Lindy.

We fitted together like two peas in a pod. Love came first with Lindy and me. The sex wasn't sex. It was making love. If you've ever had that in your life, you know that nothing else comes close. I miss her. She walked away seven years ago. I didn't take enough notice of her when she was here, and I regret that.

But life's for learning. So, out of the stupor-market and out into the fresh air. Past all the SUVs that never see a dirt road, and load the groceries into the trusty Rover. One more stop. The rubberty-dub for a slab of Cascade Blue. I get into the driver's seat and start the engine. I always start the engine before putting on the seatbelt. So, I start the engine then reach round for me seatbelt. And get the fright of my life. There in the passenger seat, is a small boy. The Rover jerks forward. I take me foot off the clutch as if I've trodden on that snake. He looks at me quite calmly. He's got a little backpack on his knee and he's hugging it with both arms. Then he holds out an envelope.

'Mum says to give you this,' he says.

I take the envelope. I'm not sure what expression is on

my face. I don't want to scare this kid. I hope I'm looking normal, but I think I've turned pale and I'm looking scared. I sense that my life has just spread out against a great wall. This kid looks up at me and smiles. He's got a dimple high up on his left cheek. Same as me. His hair is chestnut brown. Slightly redder than mine. He has a cowlick on the right side of the hair line. Same as me.

'Mum said to smile, then you'd get it.' Then he adds, 'You're my dad.' Well, by the look of him, there's no need for a paternity test.

God almighty! What do I say next? I mumble a subdued 'Hallo. What's your name?'

He says, 'I've got lots of names.' And he becomes very chatty. 'Mum calls me Little Tezza because I remind her of you. She's told me all about you and your house.'

'Well, it's much nicer now than when she lived there.' I blush with shame when I think of what she had to put up with. There wasn't even a dunny in those days. I wasn't concerned. And I thought she shouldn't be concerned either. There was no kitchen. There was running water. In the creek.

I was in no hurry. But she couldn't wait. I see now why.

'My real name is James,' he says. 'But everyone calls me Jimmy.'

'After your grandad.'

'Yep,' he says. That man had not one good thing to say about me. I guess he won in the end. And he was probably right.

So, I open the letter. I look at her handwriting and a tsunami of feeling seems to drown me. Lindy could write like a calligrapher. Perfect O's and F's and S's in perfect proportion. I'm not ready to read this letter but by some osmosis I feel and know everything that's in it. I hold it to my face and I can smell her scent. I've got no idea what it is, whether it's her shampoo or soap or simply her natural scent. But I recognise it. It fills me with longing and regret and sorrow. Lindy. Lindy! I was full of ignorance. I paid no attention to the details of her life. I was just a blind coot yelling my way through the glorious years. Drugs, sex and rock and roll. Me. Me. Me. Just the most irresponsible mountain goat that ever danced on the roof of the valley.

'She's sick,' he says. 'She had cancer and has to have chemotherapy. I'm not supposed to know, but I do. But she'll get better.'

I want to reassure him. He looks vulnerable and afraid. I want to say something like *she'll be right, son.* Son! What right do I have to call him son! I can't think of the right thing to say, so I say: 'So where's Mum, now?'

'She was over there.' He points to the corner of the building. 'She took off when you opened the letter.'

Jeez … another tsunami of missed opportunity and regret. I decide to move forward.

'Do you like dogs?'

'Oh!' he says. 'I love dogs! I've always loved dogs! But

we've never been able to have one. In Melbourne, you're not allowed to have dogs in flats.' He's talking with his whole body. He's become really animated. I'd promised meself a slab of blue, but I've changed my mind. Wouldn't do me any harm to have a break from the piss.

'Well, what we're going to do, is visit the dogs' home and find you a pup. Is that OK?'

'Oh! Tezza! You're the best!' **HW**

Cool-Climate Wines in the Huon Valley

Winsor Dobbin

The Huon Valley is rightly famous for its food and wine. Winsor Dobbin, based in Cygnet, holds regular wine tasting events and dinners that bring people together to enjoy and learn about what the region has to offer. Here, he introduces the history of wine growing here 'on the edge of viticultural possibility'.

Winsor is an experienced Australian journalist who has been based in cities including Johannesburg, London, New York and Paris. He has worked for Associated Press, Reuters and AFP as a foreign correspondent, along with reporting and editing for News Limited and Fairfax newspapers as both a sports reporter and feature writer.

A freelance writer since 2007, Winsor writes wine, food and travel stories for national and international magazines, websites and blogs and has been fortunate enough to visit most of the world's major wine regions, from Argentina to South Africa.

Making high-quality cool-climate wines in the Huon Valley is a classic case of high risk/high reward. Just a few decades ago the possibility would have been laughed at, but wines from Huon producers, including Home Hill, Chatto, Sailor Seeks Horse, Kate Hill and others, are now much sought-after by wine bars, wine lovers and retailers across Australia.

Jancis Robinson, the UK's most influential wine writer, says Tasmania has immense potential for making world-class wine – and the Huon Valley is at the vanguard as the coolest wine region in the coolest state.

'Wine production on Tasmania has always been small, but its potential is now being realised,' Robinson says, listing Huon stalwart Home Hill among her favourite Tasmanian producers.

The Huon's southerly location puts its vineyards at risk from both frosts and hailstorms. But it also has the right attributes to produce stellar wines, particularly those made using chardonnay and pinot noir grapes.

The Huon has a global reputation for the quality of its apples, pears, and cherries, but the wine industry might surpass them all in the long term in Australia's southernmost municipality and coolest wine region.

Jim Chatto, from Chatto Wines, describes his own Isle vineyard, overlooking the Huon River at Glaziers Bay, as being 'right on the edge of viticultural possibility'. But global warming and improved technology have made wines from the Huon much sought-after.

Paul and Gilli Lipscombe, from Sailor Seeks Horse at Cradoc, between Cygnet and Huonville, worked in France, Margaret River, Oregon, and New Zealand before deciding the Huon gave them the best chance of making world-class chardonnay and pinot.

'Our belief is that great pinot noir and chardonnay are made on that edge, where the risks are high but the rewards even higher.'

It pays to remember that the industry is relatively young. The oldest wine producer of note in the south of the state is Moorilla Estate, which was established in 1958. Most of the major vineyards today were planted in the 1990s or later, and most remain extremely small.

The modern wine industry in the Huon only started in the early 1970s, when Max and Lorraine Reynolds planted riesling at their Chateau Lorraine vineyard in Cygnet and Steve Ferencz bought land in Cradoc and established Panorama vineyard, which he later sold to the Vishacki family.

Eric Phillips, who had worked for the Reynolds in the late 1970s, then established Elsewhere with his wife Jette, and later owned next door micro-operation No Regrets. He also provided the first cuttings to Home Hill.

Elsewhere's current owner, Owen Knight, points out

that southern Tasmania is on a similar latitude as some of the great wine regions of the world, including Central Otago in New Zealand and Burgundy in France. Those regions are both known for their pinot noirs, and that variety shines in the Huon.

The immense potential of the Huon has drawn inventive producers like the Lipscombes, Duncan Ferguson and Susana Fernandez from Altaness at Lymington, and now Franklin-based Alice Davidson from Wines by Aunt Alice, to make the move to the deep south of the Apple Isle.

Jim and Daisy Chatto worked at some of the best wineries in the Hunter Valley and Jim was the first winemaker at Rosevears in the north of the state. In 2007 they planted a small vineyard where the couple and their family now make wines using fruit both from their own vines, and from selected growers across Tasmania.

Fernandez and Ferguson used to own Cascabel Wines in McLaren Vale, while Davidson was chief winemaker at Norfolk Rise on the Limestone Coast.

Huge strides have certainly been made since Chateau Lorraine, outside Cygnet, imported grapes from South Australia and other spots because the fruit from their show vineyard was not good enough.

In recent years, Home Hill has won national acclaim, and more Huon vineyards are on the way from Deep Bay to Wattle Grove.

Mac Forbes, a leading winemaker in Victoria's Yarra

Valley, is also focusing on the potential of the Huon, having planted a new vineyard between Huonville and Cygnet.

Look out, too, for Michael and Helen Ryder's Lower Wattle Grove vineyard, Riverbell Farm, and artist Sarah Dempsey's vineyard at Deep Bay.

There were vineyards planted above Franklin at adjacent farms Highland Brae and Wombat Springs – but sadly those ventures did not last past the early 2000s.

Among the regional pioneers were Terry and Rosemary Bennett, who received the Order of Australia for their contribution to the Tasmanian wine industry and for their service to the community. Both born and bred in the Huon Valley at a time when the landscape was dominated by apple orchards, the couple came from humble beginnings to be business powerhouses and major players in the wine business after launching Home Hill at Ranelagh in 1992.

'As far as frost goes, this side of the river is a huge risk,' Terry told local media.

Innovating and adapting, the Bennetts installed a wind machine, the first of its kind in the Huon Valley, which uses the inversion layer of warmer air, pushing it downward to, hopefully, prevent frost.

The Bennetts recall losing an entire crop to frost in 2007, and hardly any wine was made from local fruit after the 2019 bushfires left a legacy of smoke taint.

Among the accolades the Bennetts have picked up

are the Royal Agricultural Society's Vineyard of the Year in Tasmania and the Jimmy Watson Trophy at the Royal Melbourne Show in 2015. Arguably Australia's most prestigious wine show trophy, it is awarded to the best young red wine of the show.

Home Hill has had several winemakers over the years – including the Lipscombes – and Terry Bennett says it is the quality of the fruit that gives Home Hill the edge.

'They normally say 80 per cent of winemaking is done in the vineyard,' said Terry Bennett, a self-taught viticulturist.

'If you don't overcrop, and you don't get disease, if you get perfect grapes in the vineyard, it's pretty easy for the winemaker to make good wine.'

Just a short drive from Home Hill, you will find Kate Hill Wines (no relation). Kate has made wines in the US, Europe, and South America, and selected the Huon as the best spot to make quality cool-climate wines.

Kate and her husband Charles converted a historic 19th-century apple shed into a winery and tasting room and then later launched a second site, where they have established a four-hectare vineyard planted with pinot noir, chardonnay, and shiraz. There is also cellar door adjacent to an 1800s heritage-listed cottage, which also houses the company offices. Kate's husband Charles is also in on the beverage act, making craft cider under the Huon Belle brand.

The top block of Kate's winery, known as Four Winds, is planted with shiraz, which does not get picked until well into May each year. It is believed to be Australia's coolest shiraz site, and it is certainly the southernmost.

Another vineyard of note in the Huon is Heriots Point at Castle Forbes Bay, the southernmost commercial producer.

Also look out for wines from Two Bud Spur, a boutique vineyard nestled in the heart of Gardners Bay. First established in 1996, they produce a range of estate wines, including one made from the unusual French grape variety gamay.

Hartzview Vineyard, just up the road on Pig 'n' Whistle Hill, offers a range of wines, ports, liqueurs, mead, and cassis for visitors to sample. Spectacular views, wherever you look, are a feature at Hartzview, looking across vineyard slopes and Port Cygnet to the Hartz Mountains. History buffs will enjoy the self-guided walk to the painstakingly restored fruit-pickers huts that have been home to vineyard workers and their families – as well as to Italian prisoners of war.

While larger producers like Home Hill and Kate Hill have cellar door tastings on offer most of the year, many of the other winemakers are small family concerns. Some are only open on festival weekends like the Southern Vineyards Open Weekend and Spring in the Vines.

The Panorama vineyard at Cradoc is now owned

by one of Tasmania's highest-profile wine families: the Lubianas, based at Granton in the Derwent Valley. The cellar door here is permanently closed, but rising star Marco Lubiana used fruit from the vineyard for entries that earned him the national Young Gun of the Year winemaking award in mid-2024.

Some vignerons without cellar doors will open for tastings by request, but it always pays to ring ahead if you want to taste or buy wines from a specific producer.

And, of course, there are also several producers in the adjacent D'Entrecasteaux Channel, among them Mewstone, Cathedral Rock, Nandroya, Resolution Vineyard and others. **HW**

Of Wrecks and Woodchips

Wren Fraser Cameron

At Lune River, the voice of the past is always whispering – in a landscape shaped by ancient glaciers, in the way the man ferns echo the Jurassic fossils in its earth, in the fading traces of the humans who have come and stayed or come and gone. In this layered memoir, Wren Fraser Cameron examines the web of history connected to the shipwrecks off far south lutruwita Tasmania: how its threads have reached forward into her own life and helped her anchor in this place and fight for its preservation.

Wren has lived amid the bush and button grass and southern sky of Lune River for forty years. Working in community development and adult and Aboriginal education, she has advocated for the environment, arts and culture right across the Huon, distilling a message of sense of place and speaking truth to history in her work. Her novel *The Oyster Girl*, set in this same far south region, combines wide historical research with her deep feeling for the landscape and ecology of this exceptional place.

Shipwrecks lie submerged on the reefs of my imagination. Raised from the depths of history, they propel stories. Several served to pivot the plot of my historical novel *The Oyster Girl*. Set on the seas and shores of far south lutruwita Tasmania, it could not avoid a collision with the story of the wretched convict wreck *George III*: the Rock, the Great Loss of Life, the Monument. Location, location, and more mysterious wrecks were steered onto the literary landscape, landing where needed.

Since ships of change first sailed into these waters they have foundered on the rocks and reefs at the southern entrance to the D'Entrecasteaux Channel, become legend, reef-wrecks turned to place names, a rock or sea-swamped islet named after them. A colonial response to place, to name it after a catastrophe – places that had held their own names for thousands of years. Acteon Island, barely above sea level, snagged the eponymous *Acteon* arriving from Mauritius with 500 barrels of salt pork and wares from India in 1833. An abalone-rich reef, dotted with muttonbird burrows, within reach of shore; it would have called up another name.

A sunken rock only a short distance away took the *George III* in 1835 as it approached the Channel. At first gently snagged, then a sudden change of weather saw the 394-ton, full-rigged ship holed and wrecked on the rock that now bears its name. Trapped below decks, suffering from scurvy, over 120 convicts lost their lives, drowned, some shot by the British marines as they tried to escape the rising waters.

Within months the Sterile Isles, part of the low-lying Acteons, staved in the rum-barrel-toting *Wallace* on its maiden voyage as it too approached the Channel. Rum swilled over the low-lying reefs, its reek memorable. Only weeks later, across the Channel against the Bruny Island shore, the *Enchantress,* laden with importance, family silver and fine wine for the governor, was spectacularly sunk and never found, with the loss of sixteen lives. A deep southerly took the 289-ton whaler, *Marie Orr*, at anchor in Recherche Bay. Built for whaling in Hobart in 1838, the full-rigged ship had become a convict transport and then returned to whaling when she dragged anchor and smashed on Kelly Rocks. Just one life lost, but double score to the sea for taking a whaler and a convict ship.

Ships off-loading death and disease, the whalers dripping slaughter, the convict transport ships of misery, the ships conveying riches and grog – all have foundered in this small stretch of water in the far south. All with their own stories. Some stories ripple out down the ages long after the original vessel is done with them, seeping under the skin of those living in their shadow, subtly steering the passage of future lives and actions, making connections to our sense of place. We turn to them to try to understand fundamentals such as survival and purpose.

Such is the story of the good ship *Katherine Sharer*, lying for 165 years as a shattered wreck beneath the waters of Port Esperance. The circumstance of the wreck is one thing, but the story of a particular survivor reveals something very personal about walking in the footsteps of others.

It was on a storm-lashed day in Dover in the mid-1970s that I first encountered the *Katherine Sharer*. Venturing south for the first time, I had splurged my student allowance on a five-dollar crayfish lunch so large that it lurched off the plate. Behind me on the pub wall was mounted its giant cousin, huge menacing claws poised above the top-shelf spirits. Outside the bay window, a fierce southeasterly was battering Port Esperance, only held at bay by the rock fixed with an anchor purported to have come from the wreck of the *George III*. Talk soon turned to shipwrecks when a local sidled from the bar and produced a shard of pottery from his pocket. Struck by the idyllic painting scene of a fishing village that could have been where I sat but for the weather, I almost missed the name when he said that he dove on the wreck of the *Katherine Shearer* [sic] waving his arms at the window, laughing that he wouldn't do it on a day like this.

Within a few years, a dream led me to purchase 110 acres of buttongrass moorland by the languid estuary of the Lune River. On the edge of the wild places were snow-capped mountains, skirted with rainforest. South lay historic Recherche Bay and Southport Lagoon, the coastal edge of this landscape, homeland for thousands of years to the lyluequonny people who have thrived and survived here, living with the land. That sustaining web of sea and country still hangs timelessly in these places, holding the echoes and footsteps of people who have passed this way before us.

More recent, rigid evidence of pioneering settlement is everywhere. Early Europeans saw a vast forest for the cutting, pulling out the big trees for faraway wharves. Whole towns sprouted, and by the turn of the 20th century thousands of people lived south of Dover all the way to Cockle Creek. Pioneers and timber workers, felling the thickets of forest, left fire in their wake, the culture of cut and burn repeated down the generations. When export woodchips began to dominate forest practice in Tasmania in the 1970s, the demise of the small family sawmills began. By 1980 only one mill was still operating on the Lune River, producing fence palings from celery top pine. Now these wooden towns and remote mills are gone, taken by fire or the relentless erosion of the years, but the collapsed forestry tramlines, the old sunken barges, the rotting jetties and sawmill remnants whisper of the industrial times past.

The old wharf where the *May Queen* had tied up began to rot, each spring flood sending a spar or beam down the river. One such beam ran aground in the mud in the last hook of the Lune before it fanned into Ida Bay.

We used it as a makeshift landing place. Environmental and political activists from Hobart, we had chosen this large parcel of land on the edge of the far south wilderness to build community for the future that lay ahead. Other like-minded newcomers arrived, often from elsewhere in the world where the wild places are lost forever. Around Tasmania, on the fringes, more new settler communities grew, seeding hope in these globally chaotic times. A network emerged, and thousands of people passed through the Lune River property over the next two decades to attend forest and peace festivals, and music events, or to gather to plan campaigns to save the forests.

Stories spilled, by pen at first then an actual typewriter for my first novel, sailing with me to Port Davey aboard the pirate-black ketch *Wilderness*. Making our way towards the Davey River mouth, a decorative map of Port Davey unfurled, my finger hovered over shipwreck icons ominously placed where we were, when the boat shuddered to a grinding halt on the same reef that had taken out both the whaling barque *Flying Childers* and the brig *Maid of Erin* in fierce storms in 1877. Mill-pond conditions and our aluminium tinnie we had towed from Lune River saw the *Wilderness* safely off the reef with no damage.

Little wonder that I am attracted to wrecks. Outside my front window, on the banks of the Lune River, exposed at low tide, is the wreck of a nameless timber barge. On a very low tide, the boiler is visible, studded with oyster shells.

Around the corner in Ida Bay lies the hulk of the 1888 steamer, the timber trader *Victoria*. Even at my own flood-wrecked jetty there is maritime archaeology in the making, with a broken river punt submerged beneath tannin waters. We had to raise our own boat, the 1882-built *Olive May*, when she sank at moorings. After a hundred years of being a Passage Boat, the *Olive May* had an exciting new life voyaging out from the Lune River through the tricky Southport Narrows to support Aboriginal rights or take on nuclear warships or woodchip mills.

Every autumn, rearing their mushroom-cloud heads, came forestry High Intensity Coupe Burns where wood for every purpose, trashed and left behind, was torched. Bad enough that the eucalypt trees were taken for woodchips, but to leave all that rainforest understorey was a lamentable and tragic waste. Locals blockaded proposed forestry coupe burns for over five weeks whilst negotiating a Forestry Coupe Retrieval project to rescue valuable boatbuilding and craft-wood minor species. Celery top pine, sassafras, myrtle, and blackwood were retrieved from coupes both before and after they were burnt. Those were busy years, speaking for the trees, lobbying against the renewal of export woodchip licences, but together, we saw off a proposed woodchip mill at Port Huon.

Late in 2002, when we learnt the bulldozers were coming for Recherche Bay, locals quickly called a public meeting and formed the Recherche Bay Protection Group, and for the next four years all the skills and networks built up were brought to the fore to save Tasmania's most significant cultural-historic landscape just to the south. There, in 1792, the French had sailed their storm-battered ships in and stayed for some five weeks. The scientists roamed the vicinity, botanising. In 1793 the French returned, engaging in a friendly encounter with the locals, the lyluequonny people.

We drew in the World to save Recherche Bay, told every story, made art, sang up big doses of satire and history, made every connection, appealed to the head, the heart and history. Along came scientists, astronomers, ambassadors from France. 'Why Woodchip History?' asked the thousands of postcards that landed on Premier Jim Bacon's desk. 'Logging into History!' was the front-page banner for the feature in the *Australian*. We got the place registered on the National Heritage Register, right up there with Anzac Cove, on the list as one of our most important cultural-historic landscapes. We had the T-shirt, the movie. The Recherche Baybes CD. The bumper sticker 'Save Recherche Bay' was everywhere. I had a stand-up comedy act 'Celeste from Brest', a corseted 18th-century tragic in Marie Antionette wig. She was formidable. But still King Woodchip ruled.

It was in this whirlpool of woodchip that I next encountered the wreck of the *Katherine Sharer*. We attended the Australian Native Plant show at City Hall Hobart with a display of flora, picked from my buttongrass, of French botanist Labillardiere's type locality finds from Recherche Bay. We shared a space with the Tasmanian Herbarium who, with the University of Tasmania and the Tasmanian Museum and Art Gallery, were promoting a forthcoming book on the botanical history of Tasmania 1642–1820. I was taken by the cover art, the very recognisable 1792 Beautempes–Beaupre chart of Recherche Bay showing the French Garden, the *Jardin*. Then by the author's name: Janet Somerville.

Somerville was a most familiar name to me. I had spent many a holiday up country at my great-aunt Joan's in Somerville Street, Bendigo, Victoria. She had been housekeeper to the Bishop of Bendigo, but her sister, my future grandmother, had married a Protestant and was disowned by the Catholic Church and her Irish father, George Wren. Ironic that he made a shipwreck of his own family given that in the 1840s and 1850s, he had sailed the seven seas as a ship's carpenter, in ships like the *Katherine Sharer*, surviving whatever the sea threw at him. If he had gone down on one of his many ships, wrecked somewhere off Canada or Ireland or Australia, that would be the end of the Wren story. Half my house is furnished from Joan's estate; somehow, I have the bishop's blue and white meat platter. It sits heavily on my table. Atoning.

I opened the book to find the foreword, written by friend and colleague of Janet Somerville, botanical doyen Winifrid Curtis. A woman well known to me, a friend and colleague also of my late mother-in-law, botanist Mary Cameron AM. One small sentence stood out:

> Born in Lilydale in northern Tasmania in 1887, she was of Scottish descent: her paternal grandparents with their young family migrated to Tasmania in the *Katherine Sharer** in 1855 …
>
> *Also referred to as the *Katherine Shearer* or *Catherine Sharer* …

These words swirled in my head. With the woodchips. The woodchips coming for Recherche Bay. D'Entrecasteaux described vast old-growth forests 'where the sound of the axe has never been heard'. But it did not take long. The French used blue gum to repair their boats, *Recherche* and *Esperance.* Whalers, sealers, ship builders next, then the sepia ancestor axeman who cut down the giant trees for the world. When the bulk carriers came, woodchip made a wreck of our forests.

Recherche Bay was saved from woodchipping. In February 2006, history, the passion of people, and money from Dick Smith saved the day and the bay. The land in question was put under the management of the then fledging Tasmanian Land Conservancy, now a giant in land conservation.

Over the years this quirky coincidence with the Somerville name led me down a very particular pathway. What's in a name? lutruwita … old as time. Van Diemen's Land, the convict penal colony. Tasmania, colonisation advanced. Port Esperance, still wearing its French name. Dover, think England. D'Entrecasteaux if you are on a map, d'Entrecasteaux if you are French. *Katherine Sharer/Catherine Shearer*, depends on who could read, decipher accents, or set the news type. Lilydale/Lilydale, we were both born in a place called Lilydale – me on a plant nursery. Somerville/ Somerville. Been there, got that. Both Janet Somerville and Mary Cameron had graduated with a degree in botany from the University of Tasmania in the early 1940s under the tutelage of Winifred Curtis. Mary Cameron's *Field Guide to Tasmanian Flowers and Plants* is my daily companion, and has a foreword written by Winifred Curtis. Winifred Curtis's 1956 *The Student's Flora of Tasmania* Part 1 has lived, much used, on a bookshelf at Lune for years. In the acknowledgements, Winifred writes that she did much of the fieldwork with 'Miss J Somerville' and praises her wide knowledge of Tasmanian plants. Winifred and Janet, renting a shack at Southport, botanising the far south in the footsteps of French botanist Labillardiere. Footsteps we have all walked.

In 2011, the Dover History Museum asked me to produce an audio installation on the wreck of the *Katherine Sharer*. My brief was to script and record a motion-activated sound clip about the shipwreck.

Into the archives I dove, raising the wreck of the *Katherine Sharer*. Built of teak and oak in Sunderland in 1850, the 512-ton barque had already sailed the seven seas. Her maiden voyage to Valparaiso, next London to China and back, now sailing from Gravesend to Van Diemen's Land laden with cargo and Scottish emigrant families looking for a new life.

One family were the Somervilles: William Somerville, his wife – also Janet! – and young children. William, as first son, could have been Laird of Ampherlaw in south Lanarkshire but was passed over for his brother, the second son.

Fate or circumstance saw him sailing off to the other side of the world with a young family, to raise sheep – a diaspora laden with ironies. Their worldly possessions shared cargo space with trunks of doorknobs, chests of gold and silver watches, caches of copper coins and tokens, boxes of tinned herring and sardines, crates of plates and porcelain Prattware of potted shrimp painted prettily with Cornish fishing village scenes, all stacked alongside a printing press and burgeoning bags of Royal Mail. All this hope and promise stored with four tons of Lucifer matches and nine tons of gunpowder, the latter an illegal cargo smuggled onboard during an unauthorised stop down the Thames.

In the growing dark of 6 June 1855, the *Katherine Sharer* entered the D'Entrecasteaux Channel after an uneventful five-month voyage from England. Unable to rouse a pilot at Port Esperance for the unfamiliar waters ahead, Captain Thorne dropped anchor for their first night in Van Diemen's Land just off Scott Point, south of Hope Island. All should have been well.

No roads yet reached Port Esperance, only the sea. Scattered along the shoreline were ship builders and small mill holdings, a blacksmith, draper and general store, and a pub, the Freak Inn. Out on Hope Island was the Port Esperance Hotel, a fancy name for a drinking hole frequented by whalers and sea drifters. Its licensee was John Boothman, vegetable grower and lessee of Hope Island, son of a convict transported aboard the infamous Calcutta. In 1858, Boothman would bring out his two teenage nephews from Stirling, Scotland, mere miles from whence the Somervilles came.

About eleven-thirty that night, the watch roused the captain from sleep; the ship was on fire. The flames quickly took hold, and the command was given to abandon ship.

Who better to tell that story than 'Janet Somerville, shipwreck survivor'?

Opening day, and the motion-activated sound installation didn't work; I was asked to 'perform' the piece. Thus evolved the dramatic performance monologue as told by fully costumed 'Janet'. Hear the Scottish brogue, lots of rolling rrrrr's, imagine the pathos of her plight:

> It was terrible, the wreck of the *Katherine Sharer*. Janet Somerville, late of Scotland, bound for a new life to raise sheep in Van Diemen's Land …
>
> 'Twas in the dead of night when we were roused from sleep with great alarm, as the ship was on fire. Not any old cargo to smoulder but tons of gunpowder and Lucifer matches. In only our nightclothes we were put ashore on a rocky, forbidding place and scrambled for our very lives far into the dense inhospitable forests that cut and tore at our bodies. The glow of the burning ship a devil's beacon.
>
> We had made it about half a mile from shore when all Hades' furies were unleashed. The lethal cargo exploded. I was clutching wee Agnes, a bairn of only five months, when a huge section of the mast speared the very earth only paces from the

children. Unbelievable that this fury hunted us in the dark as though to kill us. We should have been dead, and the cold of the night almost achieved what the explosion did not.

When dawn broke and we struggled back to the coast, the forest hung with mail bags, the ship vanished beneath the waves, taking our worldly possessions with it. The shore was strewn with the debris of the blast; tatters of sails hung in ribbons from the trees, casks and cases rolling in the surf. Watches, scattered timeless on the sands. Fish from the very sea hanging in the branches; tins of herring and sardines peppered the surrounds. We picked over the flotsam, attempting to clothe ourselves, as we were cold to the bone and we needed food for the children, but we were without much succour on this score.

The ship's longboat took us to an island in the bay, Hope Island, to await rescue. And hope we did, most earnestly. For two days we huddled, the heavens lashing us with cold furies. When a vessel finally appeared, the Master said it was Governor Fox Young Himself, aboard the *Culloden*, but curse the English he sailed on by. Just when we had plummeted to deepest despair a schooner *Annie* appeared, taking us to Hobart where we arrived in a destitute and most deplorable state.

We were, however, greatly moved by the compassion and generosity of the people who clothed and fed us. By serendipity a fundraising event for the far away Crimean War was being held that night in Hobart, and the fundraised monies were diverted to us to ease our plight. We made our way to Mona Vale in the Ross District to begin our new lives, and my descendants live on to this day.

I oft think of the wreck of the *Katherine Sharer*, lying beneath the waters of Port Esperance. In the magnitude of the ship shattering blast, much has been made of the explosive nature of the cargo, the gunpowder, the Lucifer matches, but smaller, greater treasures were lost that night. I keen the loss of my mother's sewing box. Lost now in the shattered hold. I dwell on my Gran's baubies glinting in the dingle deep. All those links of my ancestors, scattered these long years across the seabed of those waters.

Thus spoke the first Janet Somerville.

There is no 'X marks the spot' for this wreck, variously sited by local parlance as near the Ring of Kelp off Lomas Point. An article in the *Mercury* in 1929, after the wreck of the *Katherine Sharer* was rediscovered, conflated that 1855 wreck, 'with great loss of life', with the wreck of the convict carrier ship *George III*, which went down twenty years earlier and farther south in 1835. No lives were lost on the *Katherine Sharer* when it exploded. But two deaths are attributed by association – a local woman, Mary Lovett, who was arrested for looting and pilfering of the cargo but died in custody before the matter came to trial; and a diver employed to locate the wreck in 1858. It wasn't until 1945 that the wreck was officially located. Local divers called it the Wreck of Plates for the large strew field of plate-ware and potteries. Souvenirs from the *Katherine Sharer*, before the Historic Shipwrecks Act came in, adorned the mantelpieces of Dover or got pulled from pockets to show strangers in the pub. Shards of shipwreck-china scatter these shores, some blue and white like the bishop's platter: small, everyday artefacts, sea-washed into history.

In 2017 the historic shipwreck *Katherine Sharer* came under a new threat, not of time and tide but so-called progress, lying as it did beneath the route that Chinese bulk carriers would take to berth at a proposed export woodchip port at Port Esperance. The integrity of the wreck-scape, a maritime testament to one of Dover's founding stories, needed Janet.

A timely community organisation called Far South Future was formed to save beautiful Port Esperance, the economic view-field of tourism, from a looming woodchip-led fate. There were meetings to be had, networking to be done, a community to be engaged and educated. Experts were garnered, engineering briefs and development applications digested, rallies undertaken, campaign money raised, the T-shirt made and outrage stirred that the cutting down of our majestic carbon-rich forests is still dumbed down to woodchips.

In February 2018, 'Janet' performed for the Governor of Tasmania, The Hon. Kate Warner, after she opened in Dover the Australian National Maritime Museum exhibition, *Submerged*, which included a local display case of artefacts from the wreck of the *Katherine Sharer*. In her opening speech, the governor referred to the huge keel section from the wreck of the *George III*, hoisted into the tower of Government House during construction.

The governor's aide-de-camp for the occasion was the genial Inspector Woolley, a frequent arresting officer in the past at forest protests in the Huon, protests that were all about saving old-growth forests from woodchipping.

Later, over a cup of tea, I raised the subject of the

wreck of the *Katherine Sharer* being under threat from woodchip carriers. Bold, but I was still in costume.

That 2018 Easter weekend, 'Janet Somerville' told her story to hundreds of people on the foreshore at the Dover Seafest, waving her hands in the general direction of the ghost of the *Katherine Sharer* and that phantom, the proposed woodchip loading facility.

I next took my pen to the air waves with professionally voiced and produced radio advertisements for Huon FM. Imagine you are listening as you read with a background sound montage of pan flute, breaking waves, birdcalls and a gasp of awe.

> Timeless, eh. That moment, that place, when something takes your breath away. Beautiful Port Esperance does that. And the Wow factor now underpins a vital part of the Regional Tourism Economy. That's money in our local businesses. A woodchip port would kill that golden goose. Port Esperance … a million-dollar view and it's our back yard. It's got it all: dolphins, fish in the bay, beautiful beaches, an historic shipwreck, world heritage forests all round. Aren't we lucky. But this proposed woodchip port for Dover would bring industrial noise 24/7 and an industrial view scape forever …

There goes the serenity.

There is such a rich history of forestry in our region. Don't we just love those old sepia photographs of the mighty trees, the bold axemen, the family mills, the tall ships loading at wharves, taking those trees to the world. Bet those spars would still be holding up the London Docks if the tides of history hadn't caught up with them. There is no return to the glory days of forestry, those days are past. Those forests are gone. We need to face the future now, be smart and sustainable, not dumb down to woodchips. Make those timber forebears proud of our use of the forests. Once a woodchip port is built in Dover, there is no going back …

Two days after these ads first went to air, the proposal for an export woodchip facility in Port Esperance was abandoned. Ahhh, the serenity.

When I first held a copy of my novel, *The Oyster Girl*, in Fullers Bookshop in Hobart, I was standing in front of my mother-in-law's *Field Guide to Flowers and Plants of Tasmania* and the second Janet Somerville's *Botanical History of Tasmania 1642–1820*, with its cover map of Recherche

Bay. A place saved from the woodchippers, where our footprints crossed, making meaningful and tangible links to what we did with our lives.

My own curious link to the wreck of the *Katherine Sharer* continues whenever I walk the buttongrass wilds, stooping to look at an orchid or naming the flowering *Epacris*. The gardener's daughter in the company of the botanist's son. **HW**

Midwinter

Isaac Gee

This year, Willie Smith's orchard announced that 2024 would be the last time they would host the Midwinter Festival. For the past decade people have gathered there in the depths of July to make noise and light in the dark and cold, to enjoy music and storytelling, dabble in various folk winter traditions including a giant Burning Man and, of course, wassail the apple trees to bless them for the coming crop. Isaac Gee's story describes the scene and taps into some of the ancient traditions invoked there, in a fey tale where the winter air thins to let in, perhaps, a little of the otherworldly.

Isaac is a Huon-based musician, who once found himself in an empty mall at night playing jazz to a group of people doing yoga. Finding that weird gigs are great fodder for storytelling, he was inspired to reconnect with one of his first creative loves: writing. He likes to root his stories in personal experience, and a sense of place, before gradually nudging them somewhere new and strange. He is endlessly inspired by the beauty of Melukerdee Country here in the Huon Valley: its calm, its quirks, and its mystery.

I felt a little light-headed as the applause died away and the canned music rushed in to take its place.

'Good gig!' Ro smiled and clapped me on the shoulder before turning to unplug her violin. It *was* a good gig. I'm not sure where we'd pulled that energy from, but we'd gone hard, and the punters had felt it and given back harder. We'd been swept up into that delicious feedback loop that happens so rarely at a gig. Now that it was over, I felt suddenly drained. I hoisted the bass onto my hip and looked up to see the next band standing side-stage, their guitarist looking at me impatiently, eyebrow raised.

'Sorry, sorry, I'll get out of your way.' I gave him my best apologetic smile. Caught up in the manic energy of the gig, we'd stolen ourselves an encore. *Not* the done thing at a festival, as it meant they probably just lost a song from their setlist. I lowered my head, scurried off stage as quickly as one can with their arms wrapped around a double bass, thunked my instrument down and sat for a moment, closing my eyes. Strange, this wasn't my usual post-gig high. Maybe just overstimulated. There were always a lot of folks at the Midwinter Festival.

I started at the sound of Alex's voice. 'I'm gonna go catch the wassailing of the apple trees.' He stepped off the stage, guitar case in hand. 'Starts in about ten. Wanna come?'

I shook my head. 'Nah I'm good. Think I need a drink first, I'll catch you guys later on.'

He nodded and then he and Ro headed out into the

crowd. I took a long moment to myself, then stashed the bass backstage and made my own way out into the night, boots crunching on wet gravel as I left the warmth of the barn and plunged into the vibrant colour and swirling sound of the festival. The sudden cold stung my eyes, a stark reminder of just how close to Antarctica we were, nestled in the heart of the Huon. I pulled my coat a little tighter.

Trailing along the string of light globes behind the food stalls, I heard a final chord ring out to cheers from the main stage as another band finished their set. One chord was enough for me to hear the raw folk-punk of it all – must have been the Dead Maggies. The stages would take a break now while the apple trees were blessed, then the headliners would kick off. I wanted to be back for that.

Crowds of people streamed towards those lucky trees, and I threaded through them in the opposite direction, past the food stalls and towards the cider bar. *A drink, a drink, a drink.* Hot cider would do just nicely, I thought, fumbling in my pocket for a drink token. In previous years the festival had allowed the bands an open bar tab, and perhaps in hindsight it hadn't been the best idea. If you don't give artists at least some boundaries, things tend to get a little messy.

As the bodies streamed past, I was struck by the absurd duality of the Tasmanian festival-goer. Either dressed to the nines in pagan costumes – stag horns, stilts, facepaint, mantles of fur, some of the men shirtless despite the freezing Huon air – or in the Tassie tux: black puffer jackets, jeans, and a beanie. There was no in-between.

The further I walked, the scarcer the Tassie tuxes became, and the masks and horns began to take over. Some circus act must have just finished … or the costume competition maybe. The edges of my vision blurred, and it felt for a moment like I'd walked into a Bosch painting. I was no longer seeing playful costumes, but something deeper, and truer. More *primal.* No matter how much skin was on display, none of them seem to brace themselves against the cold. I felt this strange certainty that the sanctity of the festival grounds was offering them some protection from the elements, and perhaps protection from something else as well … something far more—

But suddenly there was the cider stall, a bastion of normality emerging from the crowd, and I shook these thoughts away.

The drinks line was dwindling as punters left the stalls to catch the wassailing, that strange pagan ritual where men in funny hats shouted at trees, so it wasn't long before I had a steaming mug clasped between my freezing hands. I looked up into the endless dark of the deep southern sky and breathed in the night. Down here at the bottom of the world, away from city lights, I could so clearly see the smear of the Milky Way, and I felt that rare feeling that I got on some clear winter nights – as though the world had opened up to the infinite, leaving me just a little less tethered to the ground.

I took that first sweet sip and kept walking, already feeling better. Here on my right was the Storyteller stage: a low marquee over simple, haybale seats. It was empty now, but earlier would have played host to the poems of Hairyman, whose voice somehow reminded me of the trunk of an old tree, broad and deep-rooted, channelling poetry from a lost age of bushrangers and thylacines.

And here was a blackboard sign reading: *Next Morris dance on the Paddock, 12:30 pm tomorrow!* Ah, Morris dancers. It wasn't truly a folk festival without them, and I wouldn't have had the full Midwinter experience till I'd seem them at least once, prancing, jingling, and clacking their sticks together. *Twelve-thirty tomorrow.* I etched the words into my brain. I'd make sure I was here for it. Maybe I'd finally find out who Morris was.

A little further, past the porta-loos, was 'Wild Willie the Flaming Piano', a bizarre steampunk-looking contraption that spat fire into the air while the player thumped out a boogie-woogie bass line. Who thinks of these things? I passed it by, giving the player a nod.

So much fire. The burning of the wicker man, the fire twirlers, Wild Willie, the spit roast, the glow of the bonfire in the distance … It all felt so right for a night like this. Warmth against the cold. Light against the dark. Primal and ancient against the cold electricity of the everyday. And fire always felt communal, though I couldn't tell you why.

'O apple tree, we wassail thee!' The lone voice reached me, even all the way out here.

'Wassail!!!' The bellowed response of the crowd lifted into the night to dance among the bonfire sparks.

'Wassail,' I added softly and smiled.

I loved letting my subconscious take the wheel at festivals. There was so much going on in every direction that if I tried to be selective, I'd end up in the grips of option paralysis, pulled in every direction at once, and would no doubt end up missing all the good stuff anyway. So instead, I would follow my senses, and put my legs on autopilot – at least, that's what it felt like was happening, as I was drawn further and further to the outer boundaries of the festival.

I passed through the rear entrance – a wooden arch made of intersecting logs – and stepped through a portal out of a dream and into the waking world. I was no longer on festival grounds. The Huon Valley spread out before me, bare of any pagan adornment, but still just as magical in the moonlight. The gently curving hills, the orchards, the strange old abandoned huts dotting the landscape. I drank the last of my cider and stuck the empty mug into my coat pocket.

I looked up and my breath caught. The sky seemed to warp and flex, and I thought I caught a momentary shimmer of colour. My skin prickled. The Southern Lights? I knew they were occasionally visible from southern Tas but I'd never actually *seen* them. I squinted hard … but no. The sky was still. Must have just been the cider messing with me. The brightness of the full moon probably would've obscured an aurora anyway. But in staring intently out into the night, my gaze settled instead on an old wooden building at the edge of the field, standing alone against a backdrop of stark, naked poplars. Its wooden boards were rotting away, and in places the wall seemed to have collapsed inward completely. In the quiet of the night it looked so eerie. And then there was the sound …

Was I hearing that right? Maybe it was just music from the festival bouncing off the trees. The crossfire cacophony of different stages all blaring music at once. But … no, they were all still wassailing. It came from the old house. The sound of a piano, carried clearly across the field. A *very* out of tune piano, being played *very* badly.

I frowned. Who would go to the effort to move a piano into what looked like a broken-down old pickers' hut? An installation, maybe? Part of the festival? It must have been at least a hundred metres from the festival grounds, closer to the apple orchards. What a ridiculous waste of money to set up an installation *outside* the festival that no-one even knew was there.

Well, maybe no-one *had* moved a piano out there.

Perhaps it had belonged to the original occupant, and had been there all these long years, decaying in concert with the old hut which fell to pieces around it. I knew from all those 'free piano, pick up only' ads on Facebook Marketplace that it often cost more to move, fix up, and tune the damn things than they were worth.

Okay sure, but then who was playing it? I closed my eyes and listened to the strange, disjointed music. A melody that lurched awkwardly up and down the keys. Bent, out of tune, and punctuated with the occasional dull thud of a dead key. I pictured a splintered old piano, dust-covered and ancient, playing itself. Brought alive by the spirits woken by the night's many pagan rituals. Then, a pair of rotten, corpselike hands came to mind, thumping out a dead man's melody. That was replaced by the old, grinning face of a serial killer who lived out there on his own, luring people to the hut with his demented siren song. A chill ran up my spine. The thrill of fantasising living in a horror film. The setting was perfect for it. But I pushed those thoughts away, because this was reality, and in reality there's always a rational explanation: a possum or stray cat climbing on the old piano, or someone's bluetooth speaker they'd planted out there as part of some elaborate prank.

Perhaps it was the gutful of cider, but thoughts of the supernatural slunk back into my mind as I listened to that eerie tune wafting through the night. After all, maybe the veil between worlds ran thin on a midwinter's night beneath the full moon, and if what I was hearing *was* somehow magical? I'd want to know. Hell, why not lean into it? Suspend disbelief for a moment and drop into the fantasy of it all. I was dressed like a bloody LARPer after all: black paint across my eyes and a tangle of leaves woven into my hair.

How long had it been since I'd truly played make-believe? And not just costume parties or RPGs, but *real* make-believe. It seemed to me that the strange ability to knowingly create a fantasy, but also believe in it unreservedly, was an art lost in adolescence. Anything beyond that point was just playing dress-up, desperately trying to resurrect a magic that was gone for good.

I breathed in the icy air that rolled off snow-capped Sleeping Beauty, and smiled. Sure, you could never fully recapture that magic, but there was never any harm trying, was there? I took a step out across the paddock and looked around one last time. No-one else in sight.

Mud sucked at my boots, and a thin mist curled around my ankles as the piano drew me steadily onwards. Had there been mist before? I hadn't thought so, but I guess there must have been. It wasn't like the valley's usual fog. It felt heavy against my legs, and alive, and somehow … *syrupy.*

The line of poplars loomed ever closer, their naked fingers reaching into the night as they bore witness to the utter stupidity of this dickhead walking alone, directly into a horror cliché. I could feel the nervous grin spreading across my face. If I really were in a horror movie, I guess I'd be the first one slashed open. Someone has to be, right?

As I closed the final few metres, the dark of the hut's open doorway seemed absolute. A black hole, pulling me in.

No turning back now.

The deranged thumping of the piano keys had become all-consuming, and suddenly I felt so very alone.

Holding my breath, I stepped onto the threshold of the hut, and froze as the music halted. *Run you idiot, run!* screamed a panicked voice in my head. But I couldn't move.

Suddenly, a broad, grinning face appeared around the corner, half-lit by moonlight.

'Oh, hello!' it said.

I exhaled and let out a nervous laugh, before taking another step. The small shaft of moonlight through the door revealed a stocky fellow sitting on a piano stool. His whole body jingled as he turned it towards me. *A Morris dancer!* Even in the darkness, the white, bell-riddled outfit was unmistakable, as were his sticks, leaning crossed against the side of the piano. I smiled at him, relieved. Nothing could disarm you quite like a Morris dancer. They were just so … quaint.

'Hello!' I said back, cheerily as I could. 'What are you doing out here?'

'Long break between dances. Beautiful night, so I went for a walk and found this old piano. Wild huh?' He leaned forward and tinkled out another fragment of his cursed carnival march.

'Yeah, wild,' I said. 'You're just out here on your own?'

'Mmm-hmm. Want some pizza?' He held out a cardboard box, and I recognised the Flamecake logo across the lid. It was from one of the food stalls at the festival. 'Getting cold,' he said, 'but still bloody good!'

Do not accept food from Faeries! The sudden urgency of the thought took me by surprise. I mustn't quite have dropped completely out of my reverie of make-believe. *Grow up.*

'Ah, no thanks mate,' I said hurriedly.

He shrugged. 'Suit yourself.'

What are you, ten? I nearly laughed aloud at my own stupidity. *This man? A Faerie? Come on!*

Even as buried in fantasy as my mind had been, Faeries were supposed to be small and elegant and alluring, right? Not pudgy, middle-aged Morris dancers eating take-away pizza. But I could chastise myself all I wanted – the thought didn't feel as ridiculous as it should have. It felt almost reasonable. After all, wouldn't a fairy disguise themself as the most benign, unthreatening thing they could, using their … what was it … glimmer? *Glamour.*

Ridiculous, outlandish thoughts like this always somehow seemed plausible at night. But then, this wasn't just any night, was it? This was the festival of midwinter, and I'd spent the night surrounded by people in costume, bathed in pagan song and ritual beneath the yellowing full moon. A kind of unreality had settled over everything ever since they burned the wicker man just after dusk fall. They'd burned it by shooting it with a flaming arrow for God's sake.

The man muttered something under his breath. I tried to piece together what I'd heard, but it didn't even sound like English! God, I was *drunk*. I wasn't usually such a lightweight. Must've been the empty stomach.

He repeated the words, and they still sounded like gibberish to my ears.

'Sorry, what was that?' I leaned forward.

He looked a little sheepish. 'I said it's rather cold out, wouldn't you say? Brrrrr.' He gave a ridiculous exaggerated shiver and a little giggle. I couldn't help laughing. Morris dancers man, what a weird breed.

'Sure is,' I said. 'Colder than a witch's tit.'

He frowned and shook his head. 'Witches' breasts are *not* cold, young man.'

'Oh.' Despite how ridiculous it was, the man's reproach made me feel weirdly ashamed. 'Sorry,' I mumbled.

He smiled again and waved his hand. 'No, no. Forgive me, you weren't to know.'

We looked at each other a while then, in silence, and he seemed to squirm under my gaze. When he finally turned his head away there was a flash of— Had his eyes changed colour? Surely not. I looked again – just a trick of the moonlight.

His watch beeped, and he started, shocked, then laughed at himself. 'Well, next dance in fifteen minutes. I'd better get back to the festival.'

'Wait, didn't the blackboard say that the next dance wasn't till …'

Till what?

I tried to picture the words I'd seen written down, but the blackboard in my mind was blank. Blank but smudged, as though the words that were there a moment before had been scrubbed clean.

He raised a questioning eyebrow at me.

'Uh …' I said, 'never mind, I'm just …'

Just what? What was I? Drunk, tired? I felt like I was on hallucinogens. I shook my head in an attempt to clear it, and as I did, the man's outline seemed to ripple.

'… Ah I dunno.' I laughed. 'Doesn't matter. Have a good one! I love a Morris dance.'

'You should join us some time!'

I laughed. 'I'm sure I will, one day.'

'I'm sure you will too,' he said, and the certainty in his tone made my skin prickle.

He pushed back the piano stool and stood, scooping up his sticks. 'You sure you don't want this?' He nodded towards the pizza box. I shook my head. 'Ah well, I'll leave it here for you in case you change your mind.'

'Sure, thanks.'

'Ooroo!' He gave a rigid little wave and jingled his

way out the door. I almost followed him out and back to the festival, but my attention drifted back into the room.

I eyed the pizza box, and the pizza box seemed to eye me back. It just sat there, lonely on the dusty lid of the piano, smelling amazing. Flamecake made a damn fine pizza. It occurred to me then, that I mustn't have eaten since … *huh*, I couldn't even remember. Way before our gig, in any case. Maybe that's why I'd felt so light-headed after stepping off stage. And all that cider on an empty stomach hadn't helped matters.

A sudden hunger began clawing at the pit of my stomach, and with it came an eerie clarity. Clarity? No. *Blankness* was how it felt. The moonlight swam tight around me, and in that blankness, two thoughts crystallised – thoughts that didn't exactly feel like my own.

That it's a crime to waste a good pizza …

… and that there's no such thing as Faeries. **HW**

kunanyi, a Mighty Heart

Lisa Litjens

Hobart's mountain, kunanyi, isn't part of the Huon Valley, but of course we all know it. It's a precious thing, to have a mountain area of such peace and natural beauty within walking distance of the city. Anytime you go, you find so many people refreshing their spirits there, yet it has space for all. Here in *Huon Writes*, Lisa Litjens shares her memories of walking on kunanyi, and her participation in campaigns to fend off recurring efforts to change it.

Lisa has been a jillaroo, environmental broadcaster, writer and editor. A lover of nature, she is vice-president of Neighbours of Fish Farming and has campaigned extensively for the Western Australian and Tasmanian Greens. She lives with her partner in southern lutruwita / Tasmania, re-wilding twelve acres they share with a border collie, three ponies, chickens, and a host of wild animals and birds.

Like the first time you see snow, or the jaw-dropping expanse of trees beneath its summit, the first glimpse of kunanyi makes you feel extraordinarily small. As if nature, in all its bare bone-raw beauty, has hauled you up against the wall and sucked the breath out of you. I first stood on kunanyi as a girl of eighteen. The ice-cold clouds lay suspended below and I could almost see the water droplets, like I was in heaven, and raining down upon the earth. I saw the biggest trees of my life in Tassie. The forest out on the west coast is blue and silver and shining, the light coming from the tree trunks like a god whispering.

Every city should have a mountain

How fortunate are those who live beneath one, enjoying – perhaps without a second thought – the peaceful solemnity a mountain brings. As we swing into South Hobart from our far-southern home, there kunanyi sits, in luminous summer sunshine or snow-zenithed winter – the lungs, soul, and noble custodian of the city. Home to almost all Tasmanian mammal species and sixty-seven varieties of birds, kunanyi is a mountain for all seasons.

Some forty years later, I have rediscovered the mountain and its immutable charms. On occasion, my partner Alan and I have driven to its 1,271-metre peak. We've looked out at the dazzling view from the rocky outcrop, and holding on for dear life lest we be blown away in the gusts of ice-cold wind, we've sprinted back to the warm comfort of our car.

Not so surprisingly, it's setting my boots upon the earth that has brought back all the wonder of my first encounter with the mountain. I may have changed but kunanyi remains, as beautiful, as awe-inspiring. Halfway up, at The Springs, you will find a large map with walking tracks. They have names like Finger Post, Zig Zag and Milles Track that take you to the Disappearing Tarn, Southern Falls and The Chalet. It is easy to spend a long while perusing this picture-window sized map, with each trail as enticing as the next.

Autumn is the perfect time to explore kunanyi. A cold wet morning only lasts a short while before the sun bursts through the snow peppermints, white-trunked on the vertiginous mountainside. Button-moss clings to rocks creamy and worn with gushing water. The Organ Pipes, revealed in the parting mist, dominate the northern slope, imposing their dunnock-hued dolerite rock upon us from hundreds of metres below.

This morning the sun is reluctant, the rain becomes a soft shower, and the chromatic sky seems to lift with the mist that is rising above the treetops, revealing kunanyi's numinous quality as we walk. Brisk is my stride, taking in the gelid air, resplendent with earth smells and something like camphor. Dogwoods, tea tree, and tall, modest-white trunks glow beside us. At the culvert I'm reminded of my first visit, and the taste of pure mountain water – when kunanyi was known arrogantly as 'Mt Wellington' only, and I was yet to grow into my activist self. Far below, across the sallow-branched and verdant greens of a thousand and more eucalypts, the city sits, content under its benevolent mountain.

Two hours later, wet coats shed, we are tucked up in our favourite corner booth at the Foodstore cafe, an extra-hot coffee and two warming plates of food before us. And out the window, kunanyi bathed in sunshine. Orange and blue hang-gliders floating near the mountain's floor.

Stomperism versus Nature and authenticity

Nearly five years ago, we joined the fight to save the mountain from bus-sized cable cars and a 400-square-metre cinema-and-restaurant complex planned for its summit. It was impossible to imagine the forest above our city with monster-carriages clanging up and down seven days a week. Even worse, turning the stark beauty of kunanyi into a scar of cement and glass.

Would the visiting tourists alight from their air-borne cars, hitch their backpacks across their shoulders and walk the tracks traversed for thousands of years by the First Peoples? Would they pause to embrace the smell of earth and peppermint, the sound of water carousing down the slope, or admire the splendid russet and black-white colours of the eastern spinebill? Might 'reverence' be the word on their lips?

The industrialising of Nature, and the unrelenting march of Stomperism over authenticity had to stop! How, we exclaimed, is human acquisition given preference over a swift parrot, a Tasmanian devil or a swamp gum? To build on kunanyi was unthinkable: 71 per cent of Tasmanians agreed. Laugh or cry, we couldn't decide, when the cable car company declared it 'little more than a city park – without the park bench or waste bin'. Such hubris could only result in calamity! So we joined, my steadfast partner and I, Residents Opposed to the Cable Car, which was expanding rapidly.

The City Hall when we arrived early evening was reminiscent of the Gare de Lyon at rush hour. Wave after wave of protesters filed in, filling the lower, then the upper gallery. Greens and city councillors declared their loyalty to the mountain, engendering a chorus of raw-hand clapping and vociferous applause. By the time the last speaker rose, the great hall was thumping with 'No Cable Car!' For those who lived alongside it, under it, or an hour's drive from it, kunanyi was not to be messed with.

On a brisk morning in autumn, we set out at the Cascades to walk the track to the top of Old Farm Road. With our fourteen-month-old border collie, we strode out and up, up, along the narrow path, rock-strewn and dry underfoot, to make the aerial photograph at 11 am. We climbed higher and higher, the bush becoming thicker, the air colder. The scent of fecund earth filled our lungs. Gullies of water trickled down the mossy-dun rocks, under small bridges of stone. Man ferns struck out in clumps, their sturdy trunks reflecting our resolve. Though the air was sharp in our throats, we began to sweat with the incline and the pace we had set. Grey shrike thrushes, in the high canopies, called their distinctive, soporific song. Is there a bird-sound more glorious?

Out of the forest, lungs swelling, we saw above the expanse of vast treetops, the Organ Pipes sprouting majestically from the clouds. kunanyi's highest peak, invisible. From the track, and in busloads, the mountain warriors poured, standing out like swathes of washing lines against a new-green sward. Hundreds and hundreds, in red and blue clothing. A drone was positioned and released into the sky. With little fuss and the precision of an army, we formed our human letters: NO CABLE CAR.

'Meander if you want to get to town' (Michael Ondaatje)

Side roads, it seems, produce serendipitous meetings. We are on our way to kunanyi, via Longley, on a deliciously warm Sunday. Our border collie, now a sensible four-year-old, leaps from the car as we stop at the organic stall. In the open, sunlit space alongside the creek, we meet Rainer, tending his garden. It turns out, so frequent on this isle, that we have a mutual friend. Rainer says his favourite walk is the Pipeline Track, to the Wishing Well.

The Fern Tree road winds its way, on endless hairpin bends, round the base of kunanyi, so that as you climb, you can feel the atmospheric shifts of sun-streaked light and cold shadow. Every so often a house tucks into the precipitous slope. On a broad, radiant corner, is the sign for the Pipeline Track.

Instantly we know why it's Rainer's favourite walk. There are the now-familiar smells of luxuriant growth, mint bush, and air so sharply clean you can feel your lungs thanking you. And there is, too, the shedding of all that has gone before in a daily life of doing stuff. Now we can just *be.*

The dank, serpentine trail opens up to the northern sun streaming down on the bend ahead. Nose to the ground, our border collie gambols from one side of the track to the other. In the tops of stringybarks, yellow-tail cockatoos chatter with zany surplus energy. As the path broadens into the sunshine, we stop to breathe in the stunning view across eucalypts, chartreuse-green and silver-grey, stretching forever, down to the Derwent River.

As if formed by the pristine air, the sunshine basking the mountainside, all the faces we meet are ebullient. They stop to admire our pup. Friendly exchanges are made. kunanyi, like all Nature, wild and beautiful, effortlessly brings humans together. It seems likely to me these walkers and cyclists are also comrades who have kunanyi's back.

Meandering across the mountain, we are cognisant that immense cable cars don't meander, and they have no place here. Our fellow trekkers too would have rejoiced when the Hobart City Council said 'NO' to the cable car. And like us, they will have exhaled a ponderous sigh when, once again, the mountain-stompers launched an appeal. Back and forth. One, beautiful and wild; the other, an arrant blight. Like Barbarians, you're never sure if they've gone away.

The Disappearing Tarn: every sighting is a gift

It's been tipping down for three days. We make furtive dashes out for firewood and tending animals, only to return soaked. The exhilarating prospect of 75 millimetres of late-autumn rain is kunanyi's Disappearing Tarn replete with all that water. Our friend assures us there'll be at least a wading pool. Any reason these days to walk on the mountain.

On a biting winter's morning, we pull in at the Lost Freight Cafe, and with hot coffee inside us, head off along the Milles Track, towards the Disappearing Tarn. This visit, we avoid the well-trodden path. Still, our boots sink, squelch, and cling to the thick, muddy floor. Clarty, in Lancashire, says Alan. Slattery, in the Lake District. (I wonder, what is the Indigenous word?) We marvel at the gargantuan effort of the convicts who built this track – the impossibly smooth stone that forms its edge.

Though it's fiercely cold, a bright blue sky makes everything seem possible. We are earlier than usual, and on the track, 10 metres ahead, sit two wallabies. One hops unhurriedly over the path, and equally sanguine, his mate follows into the smeuse. Do they sense we are benign? Or do they know their superiority on their mountain home?

The track begins to incline, and twist, and suddenly the deep mud becomes stone, and rock. Now we have become mountain-boulder climbers, and every step it's critical to place your boot in the right spot. Tea tree and dogwoods morph into eucalypts, and on a plateau, across the forest of stringybark and blue gum, is the spectacular outcrop of Cathedral Rock.

Everyone, it seems, wants to see the Disappearing Tarn before the magical turquoise water vanishes. Astonishing to us, is the occasional runner, and a man with his two-year-old son; the little fellow is happily sat upon a great fallen tree, eating a biscuit.

'Funny!' says the little boy.

'Not far to go now,' his dad reassures us.

Heartened, we pick up our pace. On the decline from the rocky path, I think it *must* be the tarn, but so engrossed are we in finding our feet and avoiding a calamitous fall over sheep-sized rocks, that we miss the sign! We push on – it can't be much further. The rocks get bigger, the boulders now steel-grey and elephantine, and they are all we can see. We climb to the top of the ravine. Has the mayfly Tarn disappeared already?

Mystified, we turn back and retrace our steps, skirting our way around sparse, thin-trunked blue gums.

I am ready to give up. 'kunanyi's brutal beauty is not for me!' I say to Alan, plopping down onto a boulder. 'I don't care if I never see it – the end *doesn't* justify the means.' He silently passes me an apple, and pulls out the water bottle as he sits down.

Fortified, we start off again. Just a few metres along is the sign: 'Disappearing Tarn'. How did we miss it? Several more mammoth boulders to traverse, and there it is! More than just a wading pool, shimmering above the river-stones, and a green that's almost lurid. Conifers sprout up from the watery bed; a forest of eucalypts stands, magisterial, behind. We stretch out on a rock and watch the colours changing shape in the sunshine. We are envious of the other trekkers with their picnic, but it is enough to be witness, to have made it.

'Maybe …' I say to Alan, passing him the last of our apple, 'the end justifies the means.'

kunanyi: a mountain for all seasons

Arriving at the North–South Track, our eyes are drawn to kunanyi's snow-covered peak. Incandescent, it sits in tufts and patches and cold ledges. The Organ Pipes are in full view. *Gothic.* As if Gaudi had visited before creating his Sagrada Famiglia. It is ear-achingly cold. Leaf litter deflates beneath our boots. In an open tract of eucalypts, an industrious gathering of strong-billed honeyeaters has sallied down to the horizontal limbs – their black-and-white heads working feverishly, plucking morsels from beneath the bark.

Five years on, and the government persists in claiming kunanyi as its own – the cable car declared a 'project of state significance'. Would 'reverence' ever be a word on *their* lips?

From our lookout at the Sphinx, the pinnacle is now blanketed in fog. Behind us, there's a shining-emerald view down to the water. The sun is warm on our backs. A mellifluous cascade of afternoon bird-notes erupts from the trees. As the mist meanders across its northern slope, kunanyi, lungs of the city, appears in all its resplendence. My thoughts drift to long ago and a young woman, misty-eyed, gazing down from the mountaintop. Four decades of wandering, and kunanyi hasn't blinked an eye. It remains steadfast – not missing a beat of its mighty heart. The impudence of humankind and their misplaced desires! No cable car shall reside here. **HW**

In my homage to kunanyi, I have also, in part, paid tribute to Mark Cocker's *Claxton*, and to my partner, Alan, for some of the finer ideas.

Black Charlie's Opening

David L Hume

David L Hume's story takes us to a different part of life in the region, as he follows two wanderers into the back roads. Self-reliant and suspicious (they have their reasons), the outsiders of David's story eke out a living in the 'forests and parks, neglected graveyards, [and] lonely beaches' where free camps may be found.

David is the author of the novella *Hidden Valley; a love story* and two volumes of poetry: *Tidelines Vol. 1: A Tale of two Holes* and *The Tragedy of the Little Black House*.

He and his young family settled in Tasmania in the mid-1980s, living off-grid and self-sufficiently on Bruny Island. He holds a PhD from the University of Tasmania, published his thesis as *Tourist Art and Souvenirs*, has written extensively on ceramic art and has taught widely around the world. He now lives at the end of a small valley along the Huon River, where he keeps goats and makes delicious contraband cheese. 'Black Charlie's Opening' is from his forthcoming short story collection, *Cherrystone Lane*.

Black Charlie's guts growl, like the possum that danced on the roof last night. He doesn't gripe. He knows there's greater hunger. He's seen much of it in the corners of the world he stumbled into, not so many years ago.

Big Charlie passes him a tin mug of coffee, as dark and oily as the lubrication that keeps the old Land Rover rumbling on the equally dark and oily road. 'Next turning, pull in. Breakfast soon,' she orders.

Black Charlie is so pale he is often mistaken for an albino. Big Charlie slapped the black part on him when she told him he looked so sexy in his tight black jeans and matching body-hugging shirt that just held across his weedy chest. That was twenty years ago. Since that day he only wears black. In reply, he told her he loved her accent, born in the high peaks of Europe. He also loved her ample breasts, soon had fun with her unmissable butt and found her blue lippy and eye shadow irresistible. But he wanted to come across as a modern and sensitive man.

Since then, they've been in blissful transit. Not around Venus, or any other distant planet, but around the country and more recently the backroads of Tasmania. During this time Black Charlie has let his Mohawk grow out and the vibrant rainbow colours grizzle to grey. Big Charlie now keeps her blue lippy and eye shadow for special occasions, but maintains her natural jet-black bird's nest.

Black Charlie pulls over where the road widens, just

after a junction, just before a wide white-gated driveway that is the entrance to a paddock full of small horses and mini goats. The high roof of the camper catches a cross wind and sways. As Charlie climbs between the seats, into the back, it creaks on its springs and sways some more.

They don't speak. These are precious moments, before the little bundle of rags in the corner stirs and extends a groping mitt in silent demand for porridge. They consult the map between mouthfuls, planting fingers on forests and parks, neglected graveyards, lonely beaches and where they estimate camps they've been told about might be.

Black Charlie is measuring distance with two walking fingers. Big Charlie scoffs her porridge, sculls her tea, inverts her cup into her bowl, studies it, then points to the spot on the map that Black Charlie's finger has just stepped from. 'There,' she says emphatically.

Black Charlie doesn't argue, not because he always does as he's told but because it's less far than his fingers were stepping, and both he and Big Charlie are folk of few words. In the evenings, when folk speak most, she sews and he carves, or she cooks and carves while he breaks and trims and sews pelts together. Or they read, sometimes to each other, then clamber into the frontal lobe of the camper and make it rattle and sway again.

The bundle of rags, conceived in the bed on high and born onto the table below where they take breakfast, stirs slowly and is fed. Black Charlie finishes his coffee and climbs back into the driver's seat. They have another fifty clicks of good road to collect supplies. After that they are on the dirt and the road is clear and barren, on account of people driving more cautiously. They stop twice before the dirt to gather supplies and once along the forest track, to pick a few mushrooms and for Darko, growling in Black Charlie's ear, to take a pee.

They make camp at the end of a forest spur, where heavy boulders have been parked on a rise above a small stony creek, to keep the public out of public land. They are welcomed cautiously by others. Caution, they know, is a common state for those on the road and while they often run into friends in different camps, there are ten times as many whose paths never cross.

Two elderly women, limited in their camp by the nature of their bus, are the first to say hello. Or rather it is the equally elderly Labrador which sniffs Darko's butt.

'Been long here?' asks Big Charlie.

Millie, the heaviest, more forward and more open of the two women, tells her, 'Couple of weeks, nice and quiet,' then motions to the old Kombi in the other corner of the clearing. 'He's okay, quiet, keeps himself to himself. A bit simple, if you ask me.' She introduces herself and Molly, her less forward travelling companion.

'Oh and that's Puddle, he's old and been done.'

'Charlotte,' says Big Charlie, 'but friends call me Charlie, Big Charlie.' She gestures in the direction of the high-top camper, its vaguely military green blending in with the bush, where Black Charlie is setting a fire. 'That is too Charlie, Black Charlie and this' – she pats the Rottweiler at her knee – 'is Darko. She's not so old but also' – she hesitates – 'been done as you say.'

Black Charlie releases the chooks from the trailer. All girls. They'd had trouble when they kept a rooster. Other campers whining about disturbing the peace and quiet of nature. Charlotte usually had a piece of them, about nature not being quiet, and often added something about being 'doomed because of you people'. To which Darko always concurred, as they retreated to their own wheels. Besides, Black Charlie has come to recognise that roosters tend to gather at a lot of out-of-the-way street corners, where travelling hens pass or stop. A lot like teenage boys. And that they could be relied on to make young chicks, if kept cramped in the trailer for a week or so. But you were always on the lookout, always on the move when you kept roosters, so it was best to turn them into a tasty broth, sooner rather than later.

With the hens out foraging, the fire smoking from under damp wood, Black Charlie draws his knives over a whetstone: a skinner, a boner and a carver. He likes to think he has the sharpest knives for miles, but since they usually move every couple of days, or weeks at best, that's hard to prove.

Millie, at the behest of Molly, who spotted the chooks

from beneath her shadows, calls out as Big Charlie is leaving. She begins with a friendly 'Big Char—' then as Big Charlie turns, transitions quickly to a formal Charlotte, asking if there might be a spare egg or two and says they're happy to pay or swap some bean sprouts. Charlotte scoffs at the offer, knowing that Charlie will feed the sprouts to the chooks, but that every dollar will buy fuel.

'There may be. We will see in the morning. Dollar each.'

Molly shakes her chins in hope and agreement. 'It's been a few weeks between eggs.'

Charlie has strung up one of the wallabies they collected on the road by the back legs and is heaving off the skin. Darko is already munching on the head. Puddle circles. Charlotte lends her weight to Charlie's struggle. Soon the carcass swings naked, lean and purple.

As Charlie begins to butcher, opening up the paunch, Darko circles close. Puddle keeps a respectful distance. Charlie hooks out the giblets: heart and lungs, and tosses them to her, the liver to the older dog. They scoff their morsels in one. The carcass is soon boneless, and Charlotte is cranking the handle of an old cast-iron mincer while Charlie feeds it strips of lean purple meat. He stokes the fire and makes more smoke. Charlotte mixes the sticky flesh with oil and some yellow mushrooms.

The low rolling smoke raises the attention of the old man from the Kombi, the side door scuffing open. Charlotte glances over, with the usual caution of those on the road. Beneath wide bell-bottom jeans, that may have come from the original era of wide bottomed trousers, long dirty toenails dangle to earth. An old tartan blanket covers a pear-shaped torso, topped with a shrunken head, framed by an untamed beard and long, thin, greasy hair.

Charlotte doesn't like beards, especially long unkempt ones. She distrusts mostly bald men with beards and long thin greasy hair even more so. 'Child fiddlers', she calls them and mutters as much, missing her alliteration.

Black Charlie spits on a hunk of heavy steel in the shape of a manhole grate. It sizzles loudly; he slaps on some patties. Slowly the old man limps closer, the kind of limp the result of a thorn in the foot, a thorn that would have to fester and burst out in its own time. The old man can't reach that far and is unlikely to find a volunteer. Darko growls at every untimely step.

'Is that wallaby there on the … the … the …?' comes a hesitant inquiry, pointing, with a crooked finger to replace lost words.

'Yar,' snaps Charlotte.

'Not tasted wallaby in a long time,' slurs the grubby old man, rewrapping his blanket and peeling his hair from his face.

Charlie notices the tension. He understands Charlotte's stereotyping. 'I'll fetch you one over when they're done, old man.'

'That's very hosp … hosp … hosp—

'Kind.' Charlotte completes his sentence, slamming the mincer down on the block. At which point the old man retires to wait and Charlie has a word with Charlotte. A hundred times he's told her that in some dusty corners of the world he's travelled, folk would offer the old man food, if not shelter, and listen to his stories.

She accepts her ticking off but says she can't help it, as she has done a hundred times before, that she just has this feeling around some people, sometimes.

That evening, while Charlotte reads a book, about hermits in the outback, borrowed from one of those little free community book exchanges, Charlie cuts a cross into a sheep's skull, right between and just above where the eyes would have been. Through the gradual abrasion of bone he makes a window in the shape of a crucifix, then sets about cutting away the bone at the back of the head. He inserts a small tea candle, lights it and sits it on the bonnet of the camper they call home. The skull shines a weak light. Charlotte thinks it enough to ward off evil spirits, or filthy, straggle-haired men with bushy beards. It also keeps the possums off the roof that night.

In the morning six chooks deliver five eggs. Charlotte delivers two to Millie and Molly, returning with two dollars she deposits in a biscuit tin they keep under the passenger seat. A shallow tin, with a picture of a cute, homely cottage, surrounded by rolling fields of sheep and cattle, on the lid. She always pauses to take in the picture before prising the lid off. They know the tin holds seventy-six dollars when full. Enough to fill the tank with petrol. They're both half full.

Millie and Molly are so grateful that they perform a strange, coordinated, almost religious ceremony. First the toasting of two slices of homemade bread till they are dry and crumbly, buttering and vegemiting, then slicing into strips before, in perfect time together, beheading the eggs – since boiled for three minutes – and inserting said toasted, buttered and vegemited strips into the yolk and into gobs. The ceremony causes both women to close their eyes in blissful delight as they macerate the dark, glossy, eggy strips.

Charlotte looks on in wonderment at their deliberateness and pleasure, the simple pleasure two eggs have yielded.

'There's folk more poor than us,' whispers Charlie.

Shady is up early for Shady. Shady walks but never talks, not a single word in five years. When they are on the move Shady dozes, lulled to sleep by the mostly regular rumble of the engine and wheels turning over the road. When they aren't on the road Shady walks in the forest, around the camp, or along the beach in the morning, mostly with Darko for company. In the afternoon Shady does schoolwork. Well, he draws pictures, of what he's seen in the morning. Today he draws tall trees with a bent witch's hat mountain in the distance and a little creek in the foreground. All with thick black outlines. Charlie and Charlotte are of the opinion that if he can relate to his environment, the place where he lives, he is learning and will be alright. Even if his environment changes from day to day, week to week. For Charlie and Charlotte the most important thing is to not let him be taken away.

On the second day camp is made more comfortable. Charlie strings up a canopy from the camper, propping it up with a couple of bush poles. Charlotte sweeps and spreads a few skin rugs on the dirt. Supplies last a week, before the dried rations begin to get the better of them.

The old man in the Kombi moves on two days in, and Millie and Molly pack up the day after, but not before buying two more eggs and telling Charlotte the extensive story of how they came to be on the road. Which, in short, is Molly's sensitivity to electric light. But like the road, stories go on, especially when Milly is doing the telling, and Molly is always a long time squatting in the bush.

'You see, Molly grew up in the city but had to get out. She loved people and crowds. Just as she loves your candle in a skull.'

'Ghost light,' corrects Charlotte.

'But she got sick more and more, but the more she went into the bush the more the headaches stayed away.

No-one believed her. Some bought her curtains. But it was more than the light. It's the residue, the fallout into everything. Like the air is charged with light, long after the light has burned out. Like everything it touched. Everything it's shone upon is charged and burned.

'Molly calls it her damning. Others call it her drama-ing. Then her skin flaked, her hair was constant static and attracted to every artificial fibre. Her eyes itched and the itch smelled of piss ants. Now she only sees in pixels.'

Only Millie believed Molly. So she bundled her into the back of her camper and drove her, as fast as she could, as far as she could, from neon, far from halogen, far from fluorescence, far from optic poison, to the darkest skies in the country.

Eggs and dried beans are not getting Charlie off to a good start in the morning, and the coffee is getting thin too. Charlotte is drinking tea made from the local ground cover and Shady is drawing in the dirt and scratching trees. Only Darko is doing well.

They would have gone south to where the beaches are many and people few, where they could back into the still, damp forest, listen to the waves crashing on the rocks across the road and forage along the coast. But the crayfish season is starting at the weekend and the fisher folk, in their salt-haggard utes, leaky caravans and tinny boats, with their beer and generators, will be swamping the place. And that is going to be too much facial hair and too much thin hair beneath too many dodgy beanies for Charlotte.

The high mountain park, on the other hand, will be quiet, and the water from the river, sweet. You have to be careful going in, the track is slow, narrow and steep, and there isn't much room once you get in, so not many folk go there.

Hunting and trapping is good too, if you get desperate. There isn't much veg in the park but lots of fresh water and mountain air, which makes it ideal for drying meat. Two weeks in the mountain breeze sets salted strips of wallaby to tough pliable straps that last forever. Charlie makes good hardtack and carves bones.

Charlotte finishes her book about methylated hermits up north and together they make up stories, based on Shady's drawings, about how they live and where they live, and Darko brings home some meat, until they set off again.

As they re-enter the highway the utes and boats and battered caravans of the crayfish folk speed by in the other direction.

'End of the weekend,' chorus Charlie and Charlotte.

The beach would be okay now, but Charlie has other ideas. Continuing to where the crayfish folk came from, slowly, they meander along the narrowing road. Slowly, they gather the carnage left by those that hurried from the beach just as they'd hurried to it. Before the beach, way before, he takes a left and drives an hour in, along a rough track, through tea tree swamp that wakes Shady from his usual slumber and has Darko, even on four legs, working hard to stay balanced, until they come to a wide lagoon and busy camp of small fires, vans and tents. Half a dozen boats, of dull grey shell, litter the shore; the smell of fish lifts with the smoke out of smouldering hearths of stone and mud. Sooted children chase each other with lighted sticks and fragile skeletons.

The loft of the Land Rover brushes branches of spindly gumtrees. Half a dozen carcasses swing from the rail of the back doors, sweeping an arc of blood as they travel. The children follow, waving their sticks and bones. Flames lift in the breeze, then die in the stillness, the urchins' yells just audible above the rumble of the engine.

In no time Charlie and Charlotte set up camp. Charlie sets about the animals that have painted a bloody arc on the back doors, Charlotte lends her heft. Soon half a dozen skins carpet the ground. Charlie butchers, Charlotte scrapes morsels of flesh from the skins. Respectful dogs wait, then squabble as she tosses out flaps of sinew and membrane. Darko sits at her side, Shady wanders the camp with the other children.

The sun is low but light lingers enough for the skins to be cleaned and smeared with the brains of the same animals to preserve them. Charlotte tosses them up on top of the roof, out of reach from roaming dogs that she tossed the half-skulls to. Then she cranks the mincer handle and threads morsels of meat on sticks. They light a fire, burn it down to coals, warm the plate to a sizzle. Soon Black Charlie's is open for business, the biscuit tin is full, and just as soon, the little camp drifts away to other camps. Those of strong back and agile limb to work the orchards. Those of groaning backs and complaining limbs to do their laundry and start again. **HW**

Everywhere Else is Nowhere

Matthew Evans

To close our anthology, Matthew Evans looks back on his sixteen years in the Huon Valley and sums up his developing relationship with the land and the community.

Matthew is best known in the Huon for his *Gourmet Farmer* TV series and for Fat Pig Farm, where he and Sadie Chrestman raise Wessex saddleback pigs, milk a cow and work to grow and rear as much food as possible in ways that regenerate the soil and ensure that food can continue to be grown there for generations to come. He has written numerous magazine and newspaper articles as well as many books on food and agriculture. His latest book release is *Milk – the truth, the lies and the unbelievable story of the original superfood.*

'I've bought a house in Sydney,' my friends in Tassie hear me say. It's eight months since I moved down, from what – at that time – was Australia's largest city, Sydney. I've been living in Hobart, bunkered down in a rented corner of an overshadowed Georgian house tucked under kunanyi, Mt Wellington. My Tasmanian friends are disappointed, but not surprised. It's been a brutally cold winter, exacerbated by drought, meaning more frosts, but more clear, impossibly beautiful winter days. Tassie beckons enticingly in summer, but many who make the move can't believe the winters. A southern Tasmanian winter isn't just a bit of cold, no. It gets colder at many places inland on the 'big island', the mainland a thousand kilometres and more north. But down here, 42 degrees south of the equator, it's a bit dark. It can get a bit dank. The houses are often poorly designed and rarely insulated. Our temperate climate means winter lingers well into spring, and the cold, dark and damp can enter your marrow. Many of those who dream of moving here are gone after one winter. Some after two, or so the local real estate agents tell me.

'I'm excited,' I say, defensively, about the new place.

'Will you visit?' they ask.

'It's not that far,' I say, knowing full well that any distance in Tasmania is considered too far. Having to walk from your car more than a few steps, or having to drive more than a few minutes, is an anathema to Tasmanians.

That's partly why they live here.

'Why don't you come and visit me?' I offer, in hope. 'It's only forty-five minutes, if you don't get stuck behind a tractor.'

'Forty-five minutes? Sydney?'

'Cygnet,' I say again, enunciating more clearly this time.

'Ooooh, Cygnet,' comes the reply. 'You're moving to the Huon!'

Sixteen years later and the Huon Valley has settled well on my bones, if not always without damaging them. Instead of giving up on Tassie, I embraced it. Having fallen seriously in love with my new home I threw caution to the winds, bought a small farm, and haven't looked back. In that time Sadie, my partner, has joined me. We've had record cold. Record dry. Record winds. We've seen the birth of our child, built a new house, moved farms, been threatened with bushfires for weeks on end and watched the forest opposite die of thirst. We've reared pigs and ducks and geese and chooks. We've milked cows, culled cows, run a restaurant, gutted goats, cooked for 100 people in a paddock, stood freezing at farmers markets and festivals, and served thousands of pork buns and 100 or more kilos of Aunty Dot's cottage pie. We've marvelled at the aurora, felt the sting of the Southern Ocean and sat in awe of the rainbow capital of the world.

I didn't know, sixteen years ago, that the gorgeous angled light and the fast-changing weather patterns of Australia's southernmost state were the perfect recipe for rainbows. Low light, patches of sun and rain; that makes rainbows. And rainbows make me happy.

I was reading the other day about how so many people travel to experience awe. To see a whale (tick, did that in Tassie). Watch wedge-tailed eagles soar (tick, see that probably more days than not). To witness the Southern Lights, dive in giant kelp forests and see weedy sea dragons. Tick, tick, tick. To spot a quoll, or a devil, or a bandicoot, a wombat, or an echidna, amble along at dusk. To see rainbows. We live in awe on this farm, between the physical beauty, the weather and the wildlife. But it comes at a cost.

It's 2020. The surgeon peers at my scan, then looks up at me.

'I can fix that,' he says, pointing two fingers at my throat.

'We cut a seven-centimetre hole in the front of your neck, then push your windpipe out of the way,' he says as he gestures left with his fingers. 'We push your oesophagus the other way.' Again the two fingers pointed at my Adam's apple waggle. 'Then we go in deep.'

By this stage I'm feeling queasy. But he's not done yet.

'We take the spongy disc out, then chisel grooves into

the vertebrae.' I blanch. He pauses, then tosses a portion of plastic spine from his desk drawer, two replica bones that have an artificial disc embedded in-between.

'And then we put in this. It's amazing technology. Your spine actually grows into it,' he enthuses, as I start to reel and squirm.

'It sounds, um, risky,' I manage to croak.

'Really?' he says, more slowly, eyebrows raised and genuinely surprised, meeting my eye properly for the first time. 'Oh, well, yes, there's a chance you may have trouble swallowing again.' He fixes me with his stare. 'And people have been known to lose their voice.' He thinks for a moment. 'And I guess you may suffer from the loss of conscious control of your bowels … then there's the usual risk from infection and anaesthetic …'

I didn't listen to the rest. Though there was something about the always-present chance of death. I vagued out, until he came back to the now and reassured me with words to the effect of 'but none of that has happened when I've operated.'

Farming is hard work. You put your body on the line most every day to grow food. I know, because I've done it for the last sixteen years, using manual labour not fossil fuels to create food from our small patch of earth. I've wept, screamed, laboured and bled, and have produced thousands of kilos of food for us and our visitors to eat, and now have this lifting accident to show for it. It's the price I pay for doing the job I love. A job I think has merits beyond the stuff I grow, though this price is higher, far higher, than I'd like. I got this injury moving pig shelters.

A month after seeing the surgeon I'm taken down by the tusk of a sow to the ankle, which leads to several stitches, three hospital visits, two sets of intravenous antibiotics and an infection that proves mightily hard to combat. The gouge takes two months to heal, and it's only good to go in the week I get the new disc in my neck (and some feeling back in my left hand). To great relief, I retain my ability to swallow without pain. And control of my bowels. The sow wound, like Frodo's injury from a Ringwraith, still flares up quite often, four years later.

Pigs got me into this farming and writing life. It was two pig legs in an iron roasting tray, taken from a badly placed oven, that broke my bottom lumbar vertebra into three pieces in the early 1990s. That roast pork snatched me from kitchen work and plonked me in front of food writing for the first time. There's a lot of downtime in specialists' and physios' waiting rooms. I can thank those pig legs for giving me the opportunity to read lots of writing about food, which led to me writing recipes, then to write restaurant reviews, and now to write more broadly about food and place.

Pig legs led me to writing, and writing led me to

farming pigs. Fascinated by the flavour of ingredients, and inspired by the growers I met as a writer, I was determined to try and grow my own. Living in Sydney, in a three-metre-wide terrace house, I didn't have a garden. Just a plot in a community garden, in a church yard. My patch was grave-sized, and many things went to god there. It wasn't a place where vegies flourished. So, I hatched a plan to leave the city, and head to a smaller town. To a place where growing food wasn't impossible, or just a dream. Where growing food was a normal pastime.

Having been raised in Canberra, with its bitter winters, brutal summers, and with our family home built in a new suburb on a hillside with little topsoil and little reliable rain, I knew it was imperative to go somewhere where the growing was easy. Or, relatively easy. I looked at southern Western Australia. I looked at Gippsland in Victoria. I looked at northern New South Wales. I even considered the Barossa in South Australia.

But Tassie beckoned. I'd always loved my visits here.

I have a deep respect for the wild places in this state. On one early trip, hitchhiking through the state in my twenties, I wanted to go to Tassie's heart, to walk the Overland Track. A uni mate and I started at the south end, taking the ferry across Lake St Clair, and walked to Pine Valley Hut. We set up our tent, cooked in the hut and played cards into the night with others who were walking the track. The next morning we set off early, but we were not the first to walk up the Acropolis, a dolerite-fringed monolith. After a couple of hours I stumbled across a woman who had been hiking alone, a woman we'd played cards with the evening prior. She was lying, awkwardly, unnaturally, below a scree. She must've slipped and fallen trying to get a shot, her camera pinned under her chest. Blood, bright red and unclotted, dappled her hairline. A drop fell from her lips. She had colour in her cheeks. But she wasn't breathing. My attempts to resuscitate her failed. The ruddy colour drained from her face, the warmth from her soul. The life left her eyes as I pushed, and blew to try to bring her back, and then screamed and spat and cried into the wilderness. I spent the day on that mountaintop, until the chopper took her body down at dusk, leaving me to walk back to the campsite alone.

I know this place can kill you. And make you feel truly alive. We venture into Tassie's wilds when we can. That early experience doesn't frighten me; it informs me. I respect this land, where breathtaking vistas can swiftly become death traps, where the shores of stunning alpine lakes can play home to venomous tiger snakes. We swim in these tarns, as these lakes are known, which are often stained tea colour from the tannins of the buttongrass. Before ice swimming was an Instagrammable moment, dipping into the tarns was the preserve of the hardy bushwalker. We do it naked when we can, because wet undergarments can leave us hypothermic. I've swum in waterholes in Queensland and near Alice Springs. I've dipped into lochs in Scotland and waterfalls in Thailand. The joy of a dip in an impossibly cold alpine lake is not for the faint of heart. It is a thing of Tasmanian life that we treasure.

I'm standing near Knoppy's, more formally named Knopwood's Retreat, later known as The Whaler, the old sandstone pub on the corner in Salamanca. It's gone 5 pm on a Monday in 2009, so Hobart is just about as empty as it will be in April 2020, when the streets are cleared because of Covid. A car lazily drives past, and I eagerly look to see if this one is my lift, but it's not. Next to me, a woman stands and knits. I glance over and smile.

She sidles up to me, needles clacking.

'Are you here for the knitting group?' she says, under her breath, not meeting my eye, both of us looking into the street.

'Ah, no,' I offer, more surprised by the question than you'd think. It's a strange proposition, and one I'd never imagined coming my way. 'I'm just waiting for a lift.'

'Oh, so sorry,' she says, and gently strolls off and continues knitting a couple of metres away.

I have to find out what is going on, so I wander over and quiz her about it. It turns out that there's a secret knitting society. They welcome new members, with the code easily recognised as fashioning a scarf, or socks, or a jumper, on the street. I know the shop she stands near, a place where I pick up a hand-knitted, greasy wool vest not long after. I still use it, fifteen years later, and wonder if one of her tight-knit group (boom tish) did the work.

We now spend a lot of time with people who wear hand knits. While some think of the Tassie tuxedo as a puffer jacket, those who hang out near fires on the beach, or cook over coals, or who have been lucky enough to see the now defunct Burning Willie, at Willie Smith's pagan-inspired Midwinter Festival, know wool is safer. It's longer lasting. It's warmer when wet. We also now spend a lot of time with people who have holes in their jumpers, because there's not a huge amount of spare cash flooding regional Tasmania, and a jumper with a hole is still warm. What's more, many locals, including Sadie, are pretty good with a darning mushroom.

This reusing and repairing may seem quaint, or old fashioned. But what I love about hand knits, and darning, and where we live is that it's very real. People in this valley are usually connected to this place in a very visceral sense. The weather forecast is framed for those who are in amongst it – people on boats, people bushwalking, people with livestock or gardens. I have a theory that Tasmania's relative isolation, its island status at the bottom of the world, and its relative poverty, the fact that there isn't a lot of money sloshing around, mean we live closer to what the earth can support. We frequent tip shops. We grow food in our backyards. We preserve. We knit. Often we do so even if we can afford to do otherwise.

Local poverty, however, is disproportionate. I write about food, have been paid to sit in restaurants in our richer states where it costs sixteen dollars for a single scallop, and yet this valley, my valley, is food insecure. About one in five people in Tasmania don't know where at least one meal is coming from each week. I can list about ten market gardens growing nutrient-dense food in the Huon Valley alone, and yet many people find it hard to access fresh produce. Or don't know what to do with it once they get it. It's a dilemma we all face, and yet struggle to solve. In my time, this has got worse, not better.

I come from poor stock. On my dad's side they were all coal miners, until him. On my mum's side they were miners, then my grandparents were shopkeepers for the poor. My mother's family knew prostitutes and bookmakers, but they didn't know anybody who had been to university. Nobody had a phone at home, let alone a car. As a society, we should have moved past food insecurity in those lifetimes. But, for many reasons, we still haven't.

The tuxedo, a real tuxedo not a puffer jacket, is waiting at my sister-in-law's in Melbourne. I flew in on a Sunday, when none of the hire companies were open, because I had to work the Saturday Salamanca Market, flogging bacon and snags and ham and rillettes. The tux is a bit tight on the shoulders, a bit short on the legs and arms. It's from the cheapest hire company in town, and a bit faded. The waistband is very loose. Without a fitting, I take what I can get.

I'm in Melbourne for the Logies, television's big awards night. The Academy Awards of Australia's small screen, some say, which is always held on a Sunday. (From memory, the telly show we did about moving to the farm, *Gourmet Farmer*, had been nominated for something, but the detail doesn't matter.) A few times life can throw experiences your way that seem surreal, and should be grasped, and I never thought I'd be here. A stretch limo picks us up and whisks us to the venue. There's a crazy-long red carpet, and hundreds of screaming television fans. My mate Ross has told me what will happen. People in the crowd will call out 'Matthew, Matthew, MATTHEW,' and when I turn to face them, they will say 'Matthew, get out of the way so we can see that star from Home and Away!'

He's not far from the truth. The walk along the red carpet is strange. Famous faces, in real life more gaunt and painted, and a bit more hepatic and stretched, than they look on telly, are everywhere. They're stopping to sign autographs. Stopping to talk to the media. Stopping to have their pictures snapped. There's no reason for us to pause – me, a 'celebrity' in a show about farming, set in Tassie. A show with a pale, stale white bloke as the front man.

At the end of the red carpet, we line up. This is the pause before the proper photo shoot, where the pictures you'll see of famous people in nice suits and frocks are taken, against the branded backdrop. I'm with a couple of chefs. One famous from *MasterChef*, another for his restaurants and with a show about to air but yet to screen. And we're with a director. You can tell the directors. They're a bit daggier. A bit older, usually. A bit less photogenic, perhaps. They're more comfortable behind the camera than in front.

A woman with a clipboard approaches the director and me and offers to lead us on, leaving the other chefs where they stand. In seconds, we are whisked through a small, short passage and find ourselves in the dining hall proper, having been spared the humiliation of having to pose for photos. Or perhaps having the humiliation of not being worthy of being photographed. Ross's premonition came to pass, albeit more subtly than he thought.

Once we're inside, I look like a waiter in a borrowed suit, and I avoid people's eyes in case they want to order a drink. It's a long night, and I'm not sure my life has been made better by it.

Back home and farm living is glorious and grim and magical and hard. I spend a fortnight labouring with a fencer, putting new wire through an old hay paddock that has regrown. It was always cut with a scythe, the old-timers tell us, too steep for a tractor, certainly the smaller tractors that most apple growers used back then. By the time I got there, the paddocks were tall with wattle trees, but grass grew between them still, and it gave us more space for our dairy cow. Our pigs. Our sheep.

We realised, though, that we'd outgrown our hobby farm. So, we invested in a patch of land over towards the Huon River: 70 acres of gully, with some long grass, some moss, a bit of neglected orchard and loads of potential. For five years we commuted, milking cows and rearing pigs at what we ended up calling Fat Pig Farm. Fencing, building irrigation, erecting sheds, establishing a market garden. Today, that farm is our home, complete with a purpose-built dining room that we ran as a soil-to-stomach restaurant for over seven years.

Every day I say a quiet thank you to the local builders, Andrew Gill and Phil McLeod, for the house we live in, the restaurant they built. We put our trust in a very new company, and they surpassed expectations. We enlisted a boatbuilder, Dave Golding, to make our kitchen, and the timber work is extraordinary. We worked with ceramicists Zsolt Faludi and Nanna Bayer to hand press the kitchen tiles. Each day the things we see, touch, and live in and on remind us of our connections – sometimes fleeting, sometimes longstanding – to the people and place that nourish us. The Watsons milled the timber for our house and dining room. Anthony Pepper dug in the irrigation pipes. Marty Brereton milled a tree we felled and used for sheds, and shows up every year to cut hay. And we see the connections running further. Matt Tack and Coreen Ung came to us as volunteer workers, and now run the very successful Our Mates Farm in Geeveston. Cassy Faux did a lot of shifts in the kitchen and now has her own wine bar, Harvest and Light. There are too many connections to mention here. Our staff have become our friends in many cases. Our community has grown as this place has grown on us.

It's 2016, and I'm in the post office.

'Happy birthday, Matthew!' they wish me. 'It's a big one, isn't it?'

I wonder how they know, when birthday cards are a thing of the past. You do get used to people knowing things about you in a small town. And being recognised. If strangers say hello to me in cities, it's because they may have seen the television show we did. In our town? Everybody is famous because we all seem to know each other and wave to each other all the time. Faces become familiar with time, even if we don't know each other's names. We see our community at the bakery. At the servo. Election days involve a commitment of a couple of hours because you run into so many people you know. There's no such thing, ever, as a quick trip to the IGA. It's the benefit, and sometimes curse, of small towns, that people often know your business.

I collect my mail and head home, wondering how the post office knew I'd turned another decade older. Until I discover the government has also sent me birthday wishes. They're wishing that I do the bowel cancer screening test they send to all of us once we turn fifty.

I have stumbled on this land. I have wept here. I have witnessed the births and deaths of our animals, the making and breaking and regenesis of our garden. I still don't know the names of all the plants that grow here, the birds that nest and fly over here. But this place is sitting more easily on us now. When we pace this land, we think of the melukerdee, the Huon River people who have walked this land for 43,000 years (and counting) before us. We think of how we can look after this landscape, grow food and build biodiversity and soil health. And honour its long human habitation.

In early 2024, Sadie and I took ourselves off to another place. Just for a week. We walked sections of the Larapinta Trail, a startlingly beautiful track that stretches west of Alice Springs in Tjoritja, the West MacDonnell Ranges. The colours are striking, the plants unfamiliar. Fist-sized puffballs pushed up through the dusty red earth. There was little insect life and a lot of what we would think of as desert, even though it's not classified as such. We puzzled over how the plants grow in such a climate, in such heat and sun. There were few mammals, and most were tiny. Where our moss-fringed gullies are full of pademelons and bandicoots and frogs, this landscape seemed eerily empty, and strangely foreign. It isn't either of those things, really, but it isn't home. I was reminded of what James Rebanks, a shepherd from the UK's Lake District, said once about his place in the world. Everywhere else is nowhere. It's nice to see other places, to enjoy their differences, but what runs deep is what matters more.

While our connection to southern Tassie is relatively new, and fleeting in a geological sense, or an Indigenous owner's sense, we feel like our roots have grown, that we are becoming part of this place. That it sits on us, as we sit on it.

We have tried to tread softly on this land. But sometimes we've trodden on toes, often without knowing it. We know that filming a television show, and running a business, has meant we have been busy. Sometimes we've forgotten our manners. Every time a series of *Gourmet Farmer* went to air, we were apologising for our, and the production company's, lack of grace. Things have moved fast this last decade and a half. Often too fast, and we've not kept up with the necessary explanations and interactions. The upside is that we've also got a lot done, and we hope our indiscretions are forgiven.

Our community has been very kind-hearted. They've helped us keep tourists away from the farm when we're not open, and always with good grace (all credit to those at the top IGA, in particular, thanks George and Saydeh). They've been there in crises and for parties. From my second week in the Huon, when I relied on a local chef to keep my week-old chicks alive after we went away filming, to those who helped us nurture the garden during Covid by working for food, we've been the beneficiaries of a remarkable group of people in a remarkable part of the world.

I've learned deep lessons from living here. I've learned that Huon pine burns with a green flame, apparently, from old-timers who have their own regrets. I've learned that I really am a rubbish catcher of fish. I've discovered my limits, which are many, and my skills, which are too few for farming. And I've discovered that the best type of community is one that relies on each other. One that laughs and cries together in equal measure. We value the knowledge that resides in these hills, the wisdom that abides here and continues to visit or moves through the valley.

We are becoming elderly on this patch of earth. Nearing sixty years old, with a child in his mid-teens, we boast increasingly sore backs and almost entirely grey hair. (Well, at least I do. Sadie's is darker.) We are also proud of what we do, in ways that many would think of as small, or of lesser value. We have produced up to ten thousand meals a year from the food grown on this farm, and served them all on site, many to our family and comrades. We have brought visitors to this valley to hopefully appreciate just a fraction of the pleasure it gives to locals. We store about a hundred tonnes more carbon than we emit each year, while still producing nutrient-dense food, and all the while increasing biodiversity. We know our time as custodians of this land is short, but we know that what we do has more than just purpose. It has meaning, which is about all one can hope for in the time allotted to us. That, and something good to eat. **HW**

Thanks to our Major Kickstarter Supporters:

CUCKOO etc

Cygnet Garden
Larder

Thanks to our Individual Kickstarter Supporters:

Chris Waldock
Antony Taubman
Sarah Annesley
Carla Baglieri
Margot Ayres
Tansy Rayner Roberts
Cynthia Wang
Jacqueline Page
Deborah Wace
Michael Gissing
Jacq
Kylie Rankin
Cassie
Donna
Joshua Cooper
Lucas Zinsstag
Ruth Amos
Tom Holder
James 'The Great Old One' Burke
Kelly
Dani Elle
Melissa
Tim Jarvis
The Woman Booker Prize Club
T Hoar
Jo Matthews
Stephanie Williams
Karen van den Bosch
Heather Catchpole
Lisa Montgomery
Anne BC
Sadie Chrestman
Gemma Chilton
Narrelle M Harris
Susanne Becker
Jeremy Kirkwood
Patrick Gee
Wren Fraser Cameron
Maggie Harris
David Hume
Adrianne Waterman
Amber Leighton
Nigel Leadbitter
Christine Klimek
Kay
Paul Corbeil
Axel Kallesøe
Simon Crerar
Ezra Thomas
Heather McCabe
Louise Mace
Tara Marlow
Rosemary Gardner
Carolyn Davidson
Susie Greenhill
Greg Campbell
Trish Tinkler
Kelly McMahon
Rowena Beresford
Richard O'Shea

www.ingramcontent.com/pod-product-compliance
Lightning Source LLC
Chambersburg PA
CBHW030411120726
47904CB00007B/2237

* 9 7 8 0 6 4 5 9 1 3 7 9 8 *